A Comprehensive Guide to

Arrest and Detention

STEPHEN WADE
AND STUART GIBBON

Straightforward Publishing
www.straightforwardco.co.uk

British cataloguing in Publication Data. A catalogue record is available for this book from the British library.

978-1-913342-51-7

Printed by 4edge Ltd www.4edge.co.uk
Cover design by BW Studio Derby

CONTENTS

INTRODUCTION

This book is a natural progression from our first two reference works, detailed below, and provides something we feel fills a gap on the shelf of the crime writer or reader. The aim was to provide a short guide which would deal with two specific subjects from both the police procedure viewpoint and from the position of a crime historian.

The rationale behind this is simple: the book provides a readable, lucid account of each subject in a manner very different from a book of law or a procedural manual. Students of legal history will want to read this in addition to the standard works, and the general reader will find here a mix of informed guidance on actual policing alongside some narratives of dramatic cases from history.

It is impossible in the space allowed to cover the entire historical development of criminal law in England of course, but we see the book as a starting-point, something to give a taster, as it were, while at the same time being thorough in the treatment of the subjects involved.

The Authors

Stephen Wade
Stephen's varied working life includes time in offices, on building sites and in retail clothing, but eventually he decided on teaching as a career and became a lecturer in English in further and higher education. In his last years

teaching at university, he was a part-time lecturer at Hull. After leaving his full-time posts, an opportunity came to work as a writer in residence in prisons, and he filled that role in three prisons, starting with a stretch of three years at Lincoln.

He became a crime historian after discovering an interest in local and social history, and after producing a number of books, he joined with Stuart on their works for readers and writers of crime, in both fact and fiction. Hence, Stephen is the historian and Stuart the professional detective. The aim in the historical material is to invite the reader to go further and deeper into the state of the law in years gone by.

In addition to his writing, Stephen acts as adviser to television productions on criminal matters, featuring in the BBC series *Murder Mystery and My Family*, and on Channel 5's *Inside Wormwood Scrubs*.

Stuart Gibbon

Stuart Gibbon travelled south from his native north-east to join the Metropolitan Police as a teenager. He successfully completed a tough 16 week training course at Peel Centre in Hendon and in September 1982 was posted to Wembley Division as Police Constable (PC) collar number 727. He worked as a uniformed response officer before becoming a detective and qualifying as a Sergeant. In the year 2000 he transferred to Lincolnshire Police where his career continued to develop. He served as a detective at every rank from Constable to Chief Inspector, during which time he became a Senior Investigating Officer (SIO) leading murder investigations. As a DCI he was seconded to the newly-formed East Midlands Special Operations Unit (EMSOU) as one of a small number of SIO's in charge of murder and kidnap throughout the five East Midlands police forces.

Following a career of more than 30 years Stuart made the decision to retire from the police service. He is now a writing consultant (GIB Consultancy) who advises authors to ensure their police procedures are accurate and authentic. He also appears on TV and radio as a policing expert and features in true crime documentaries about historical UK murder cases including *999:Killer on the line* and *Deadly Women*.

Our books

Our first book *The Crime Writer's Casebook* was published in December 2017. Although there are many true crime books in circulation, we believe that the *Casebook* is unique in that it looks at crime from both a historical and contemporary perspective. From the chaotic murder scenes of centuries past to the modern technology now used to track down the killer, the *Casebook* has proved hugely popular with the crime community, both writers and readers alike. If you're an aspiring or established writer looking to get your facts right then this book would be a useful addition to your bookshelf.

Book 2 *Being a Detective* is focused on the role of the UK detective, from the creation of the first professional detective department in 1842 to modern-day crime investigators. This book, published in March 2019, contains a wealth of information about the history and evolvement of the detective. Like its predecessor, *Being a Detective* contains true crime case studies and clear explanations for context. Summarised as *An A-Z Readers' and Writers' Guide to Detective Work Past and Present,* the book is presented in an alphabetical format with over 100 individual subject entries. From the **ABC principle** of crime investigation to **Zombie knife** this book is an essential companion for true crime fans.

The authors have now decided to look more closely at certain individual aspects of crime, the law and police procedure, with the publication of a series of comprehensive guides. These guides are intended to improve the readers' understanding of the subject area, whether criminal offences or the procedures involved during their investigation. They will provide you with a unique insight and take you behind the scenes to hear first-hand accounts from historical and modern-day policing.

Neither Stephen nor Stuart is a lawyer qualified in criminal law, but they both have considerable lifetime experience which enables them to speak with authority on the subject of true crime. The combination of a seasoned crime historian and an experienced former police detective will hopefully provide you with an interesting and informative read. They hope that you enjoy reading this guide and thank each and every one of you for your support.

Part 1

ARREST

'In taking a prisoner to the police station no unnecessary Violence should be used, nor should the handcuffs be put on unless there is a real need for same...'

Constabulary Instruction Book, 1920

Introduction

In television soap operas, police officers tend to arrive at characters' homes with alarming frequency, and they appear to take delight in arresting someone with an accompanying sense of foreboding. Viewers could be forgiven for assuming that an 'arrest' is the same as a charge, because the poor arrestee tends to shiver with fear, and then be carted off by a burley police officer, to be grilled in a cell and accused of something unspeakable. Of course, an arrest is not an occasion on which a person is charged with an offence. It is the restraint of a person, with an expectation that he or she will do as the law requires.

The arrest itself does provide a prelude to the detention of the person constrained; as the press usually tell us, someone is 'helping police with their enquiries.' For readers and writers of crime narratives, an arrest is an essential part of the story, and in many dramas and novels, there may be an arrest at the very centre of a suspect's character trajectory in the tale.

The word carries associations that carry into humour and satire, as it often has the kind of comedy we relate to in popular crime narratives. The writer and vicar Sydney Smith was thinking of this when he wrote, 'When a man expects to be arrested, every knock at the door is an alarm.'

Even within the police, the question of who does the arresting has been important in the past. In 1940, in wartime Britain, special constables were recruited and were desperately needed to swell the ranks when so many had joined the services; handbooks were written and circulated for these officers, such as one written for the Doncaster Special Constabulary, and that handbook had to deal with the tricky question of 'powers of arrest.' This section of the text gives away the necessity to explain, with caveats, what to do: 'An arrest should never be made unless the person or Constable making the arrest is first satisfied that he is entitled to make that arrest. Unnecessary arrests should be carefully avoided as it will be found in many instances that it is better to proceed by summons even though the power of arrest is in force.'

But the notion of arrest is a concept existing right at the heart of liberty, the social contract and the functioning of law and order in a state. It relates to rights, to civilised behaviour, to proper process and most of all, to the generally acknowledged acceptance that law in action should be on the side of right and justice.

As I write this in 2020, the dominant media story around me is the arrest and unlawful killing of black American George Floyd, in Minnesota. The police officer leading the arrest of this man appeared on film pressing on the neck of his captive. Not only does this provide a brutal affront to the civilised values of American democracy, but it also gives a shameful impression of the abuse of police powers when arrest is carried out in such a savage way.

Throughout history, there has always been contention regarding methods of arrest, in all kinds of societies across the world. For an officer of the law to apply force on arrest, even before a charge is stated, every word and action he or she gives will be judged on the basis of what proper moral behaviour is expected of a person with such a position of power. History shows us a myriad of instances of such brutal arrests, which reflect on the nature of the force of law at each period in time.

Historical narratives of all varieties represent a range of actions and attitudes of arresters towards arrestees; the situation shines a light on a nexus of power. The power exerted by arrest is a living demonstration of why and how the law at a certain time works as it does.

For these reasons, looking at and understanding arrest with a historical perspective helps in an appreciation of concepts of individual rights as well as giving insights into how shifting circumstances change the working of law.

A glance at British society in time of war, social unrest and disorder soon opens up the real importance of arrest as a topic in law. One notable example of this has to be in the first years of the nineteenth century, when Napoleon was massing troops across the English Channel, planning an invasion of England. British observers of Europe at the time had already seen the Reign of Terror and the mass executions of aristocrats and others; they had seen liberty curtailed, and they had seen anarchy. In such a context, British radicals at home would be looked on with fear, and paranoia would rule the show. The law would play its part by coming down hard on such problem citizens of the land.

Hence, concepts of treason and sedition would be backed up by extreme emergency measures. Individuals would be likely to find themselves arrested at home or in the street and taken to a place of confinement for questioning. There would be by-passing of normal procedures on the part of the authorities, and those under suspicion would be soon in custody. Arrests in that context would mostly involve physical restraint, of course. Looking at the history of arrest therefore opens up some major questions. How have individual rights been handled? That is at the centre of enquiry. But also, has there been any legal education for ordinary folk? No. The facts are plain. Through the centuries since the Anglo-Saxon centuries, when local methods of law enforcement existed openly and were generally understood, to the establishment of the first assizes, the ordinary citizen was without any real protection from abuse.

Today, when we reflect on how criminal and legal subjects are handled in popular culture and narrative, there is almost always some distortion and misrepresentation. What persists is the kind of image we see in Victorian publications such as *Punch*, in which rogues are grabbed and taken off the streets by burley police officers. The impression often given in these is that a hand goes on a shoulder and the arrest happens with very few words and nothing about rights.

What has to be admitted is that the notion of an arrest is there in the word's etymology. This is in Latin: *ad-restare* – to stand still. The standard dictionary definition is exemplified by the Chambers Dictionary: *To bring to a standstill, check; to seize; catch; to apprehend by legal authority; To seize by warrant.*

It is interesting that the element of 'seize' is included, as opposed to 'bring to a standstill.' There is a notable difference here. In today's society, that link, the relationship between *stop* and *seize* is increasingly problematic. It was arguably simpler in past times. When the forces of order saw that there was a need for pragmatic action, they generally took it. One of my case studies in the following pages concerns the radical M.P. and reformist, John Wilkes. When he was arrested, to be charged with seditious libel, this is what happened, in the words of Lord Denning:

'In the morning of Saturday 30 April, they [the King's Messengers] went to his house in Great George Street... They searched his premises. They got a smith who broke open the locks of the drawers. They swept up all his papers, put them in a sack and carried them off...'

For centuries, then, the word 'arrest' instilled fear in the ordinary citizen; he or she had no knowledge of legal procedure. There were people above them in the social hierarchy, and those people had a great deal of power. The social stratification of British society, stretching way back to the manorial organisations, meant that the world was regulated by a proliferation of courts, and it is with the creation of courts that an enquiry into arrest must begin.

One example of a court- one that will show the heart of the problem – is the Court of the Verge. There was a court of the Marshalsea of the Household since Tudor times, and it existed to deal with the domestic servants around 'the verge of the court' which was defined as being 12 miles from where the King was located. By *c.*1600 there was a need for a specific court, distinctively different from this court. This is how the Court of the Verge emerged. It existed only until 1630.

The twelve miles in question, located around Westminster, involved areas outside the influence of the City of London. We have to conclude from this that for centuries, there were court systems which were made ad hoc, on a pragmatic basis. My historical summary will begin with an attempt to explain these courts and to stress just how easy it was to arrest a person. The only proviso, reaching back to Magna Carta in 1215, was that the King was at the very top, in the most superior court, and other courts worked by his prerogative.

Before we are too carried away by the thought that warrants would put right any abuse, anywhere in the land, we have to consider the power-base for law at local level. In the 1890s, Dr Latimer, Yorkshire historian, studied this subject in the reign of Edward I. He wrote, discussing Edward's creation of a Special Commission to investigate who had manors- where and by what right. Latimer noted, 'The questions to be put were some forty in number... The juries were to state who usurped the rights of the King by holding their own courts, issuing their own writs, and hanging offenders up on their own gallows.'

Latimer provided a list of the locations of gallows as returned by these juries. The date concerned here is the early 1270s, and at that time, according to Smithy, there were 41 locations with gallows in use in the wapentakes, hundreds and liberties of Yorkshire. This is simply one county, and the gallows in these locations were mostly multiple. The wapentake of Holderness had three gallows, for instance, and there were four in York if we include Ainsty. Wapentakes and hundreds were the establishments of groups and areas which would be regulated by locals; the liberties were quite a different concept. A liberty, in the sense that annoyed Edward I, was a collection of manors with crown franchises. Above the sheriff's reach, these manors could issue their own writs.

It is difficult to overestimate the power of popular narrative, though. Film and television in their early years, dealt with the medieval period in a whimsical and distorted way. Much of this visual narrative would have us believe that an arrest was final, and that there was no such thing as a fair trial or even a regulated process of law.

In contradistinction to this, however, we have the

explorations in more serious genres into personal freedoms and rights. The following sections will take into account the complexity of the law in terms of liberal philosophies and in the transition over the centuries of the notion of the 'self.'

Until the seventeenth century, when the Reformation and the rise of empires and massive global business enterprises had utterly transformed ideas of the self, and the notions of individualism, the person had only the rights given to him or her as a subject of the Crown. That was flexible, always vulnerable, and often ignored. Consequently, in my historical survey, huge historical events will always impinge on the structures of the law and of how courts were constrained or at least restrained, with the notion of personal rights set against the power of those who had the wealth and clout to dominate a situation.

Another basic concept is the person who arrests. The crucial factor here is the warrant, and arrest with a warrant is completely mainstream legal process, whereas an arrest without a warrant usually relates to a completely different basis of that 'stop or seize' action. Before the Normans the Anglo-Saxon thinking was always related to a communal responsibility to control and suppress wrong-doers. Consequently, an arrest either on suspicion or after an offence was a joint responsibility, although of course a person was chosen to take the lead.

The historical survey now will begin with the basis of arrest in British law: the *writ and the warrant.*

Historical Perspectives: Stephen Wade

Before dealing with writs, the first task is to trace the establishment of the King's Bench court, because that court became the ultimate primary executor of the supervision of writs.

In John Moore's *Portrait of Elmbury* (1945) the post-war world was eager for some reminders of the quintessential English virtues found in the tightly-bound and self-supportive community of the small town. Elmbury, a fictional representation of Tewkesbury, as Moore presented it, is given every element of minor transgression one might imagine, as so many people in the book are shown as existing in poverty. Many are leading lives of petty crime, but there is one account of an attempted suicide. At that time, suicide was a felony – a serious crime.

Moore had a character called Reuben, who gives an account of the suicide:

> *'Then come cryin' down to me wiv his hand all bloody. Fair turned Me up it did. I bound it for 'im....I sent for the policeman and he Took him away....'*

Moore adds: 'Yes, I suppose there ought to be a charge rightly. We contrive our world in such a fashion that a desperate man prefers to take his leave of it: and we are so shocked at his dislike of our beautiful world that we call him a criminal.' It took until 1961 before the act of suicide was no longer a crime.

The little story in Moore's book illustrates, though in a modern context, the nature of the 'common law' which has been in communities from way back, through the pre-Norman centuries. The local community deals with an incident, and the seriousness of it is weighed and considered, along with the aim of taking it further or not. This must have been the case in the Anglo-Saxon world, which was run by the 'hundred' and the shire court. As John Richardson explains in his reference work on local history, *The Local Historian's Encyclopaedia*:

'Hundred courts appeared in the 10th century. A hundred was an area of Administration between shire and parish. The courts were essentially folk-Moots, presided over by the hundred bailiff, and met, at least in Saxon times, monthly. The comparison with shire courts which by an ordinance of King Edgar met only twice a year, indicates the greater importance of the Hundred courts at this period.'

These examples of instant and close-up justice are given in order to introduce the notion of the Common Law. This is important for the notion of arrest because of course the act of arrest, and who it is enacted by, and by whose order, under what power, is at the heart of any criminal law. A century ago, in a major work of medieval history by Kenneth Vickers, *England in the Later Middle Ages*, we have this, referring to the reign of Edward I in the late thirteenth century:

'Arrangement and definition were the two great objects of the lawyers of the time, and in carrying them out they produce the Common Law of England, which was to be the most characteristic product of the English race.'

The facts are far more complex than that, although in essence the period referred to is right. The relevance here is that the Common Law, with its awareness of the weight of custom and 'what was always done' in assessing a potential crime, always had to deal with the issue of what was to be done with a transgressor?

The important historical development here is the confrontation between past practice and current society and ideology as the Norman conquerors knew it after 1066.

A fruitful place to begin here is in some explanation of the Common Law. A P Herbert wrote that, 'The Common Law of England has been laboriously built up about a mythical figure – the figure of "the reasonable man."' But there is more to it than that. The beginnings of arrest as a central concept in law and individual rights are in the fusion of the traditional structures and customs in pre-Norman society in England, with the courts and trials of the society that William I and his successors framed.

J H Baker, the celebrated legal historian, gives us a clear and capacious account of the origins of Common Law in his magisterial historical work (see bibliography). This law came into full understanding and acknowledgement in the twelfth century; before the development of the assize system, as Baker makes clear, there was the creation of one of the most important works on law in England: this is a treatise on the laws and customs of England by Sir Ranulf de Glanvill, who was *justiciar* of England 1180–1189). The justiciar was the most important law officer, standing as the King's first adviser and administrator in legal affairs.

Baker explains Glanvill's importance:

'The great step forward was in the author's treatment of the fixed customs of the King's court as constituting.... the law and customs of the realm....Glanvill and his fellow

councillors under Henry II produced a coherent system of
English law deriving ultimate authority from the King.'

Justice given ultimately by the sovereign gradually became the dominant arm of the law, above the local procedures and attitudes. For our purposes, the most important development is the creation of the 'Bench' – the King's court, along with the travelling version, the eyre, and later the assize. There were initially courts at which the King was present, and which followed the King, and then there were courts who stood with the King's authority. By the middle of the thirteenth century, Baker explains, '...it is possible to perceive the origins of the two principal courts of common law, the Common Bench and the peripatetic court *coram rege*, or King's Bench.' *Coram rege* refers to hearings before the King himself.

Of course, in the midst of all this change towards the end of the thirteenth century, there had been later versions of Magna Carta and the statements therein relate very closely to the present discussion. In the text from 1215 we have:

'In future no official shall put anyone to trial merely on his own testimony, without reliable witnesses produced for this purpose. No freeman shall be arrested or imprisoned or deprived of his freehold or outlawed or banished or in any way ruined, nor will we take or order action against him, except by the lawful judgement of his equals and according to the law of the land. To no-one will we sell, to no-one will we refuse or delay right or justice.'

The words are very grand, but notice the importance of 'freeman.' This was a lord's tenant on a manor, one who worked with a set rent. It omits the poor villain who only had the sweat of his brow and the strength in his muscles to offer. He was excluded here.

There were then, from the thirteenth century, the beginnings of the assize system. This meant that there would be a proliferation of courts across the land. The idea was revolutionary really: to have a circuit of court sessions, adjudicated over by one of the King's justices, and over the days of the hearings, all awaiting trial would be dealt with. That meant clearing the jails of those charged, and dealing with any other affairs which had been suspended for whatever reason.

The end of the assizes came with the legislation of 1971 forming the crown courts. A report of 1969 had recommended 'that a new superior court of criminal justice be created to be called the Crown Court which shall absorb the criminal jurisdiction at present exercised by Courts of Assize and Quarter Sessions...'

We could summarize the other courts controlled in various jurisdictions, in this way:

The King's Bench
The assizes (where justices heard cases on circuits across the country)
Manorial Courts (Baronial courts and the leets)
Church or consistory courts
The local magistrates' courts/ quarter sessions

Through the Middle Ages, in that long adaptation of law to the changed society which existed from 1066 through those centuries in which French and English mixed, the law and related documentation was most often in Latin, or in Norman French. An interesting insight into the situation is possible when one reflects that the 'father of English poetry,' Geoffrey Chaucer, was the first poet to write in English, producing his *Canterbury Tales* in the 1380s. One of the acts of imagination required of the social and legal historians here is to envisage a situation in which the ordinary subject, who would speak English, encounters law in a foreign language or languages. Just as the Bible was in Latin until the translation was printed in 1535 (written by William Tyndale) so the legal tomes would be in the language of scholarship, and so the distance between everyday worker and the establishment would be immense and intimidating.

Now we return to the question of writs. The legal definition, as in Mozley's *Dictionary of Law*, is: 'The sovereign's precept, whereby anything is commanded to be done touching a suit or action. Writs were distinguished into original and judicial writs. Original writs were those that were sent out for the summoning of a defendant in an action...Judicial writs were sent out by order of the court where the cause depended...'

This division of writs becomes very important in understanding the workings of arrest and the following topic of detention; the important factor here is that a prerogative writ, issued by the Crown, became the judicial writ which countermanded court decision, but equally, a series of writs could call judicial officers to account, if suspicions of wrong-doers from them had been aroused.

Arrest and Writs

By the time of the Reformation and the arrival of the Stuart sovereigns, as J A Sharpe has pointed out, something of great significance regarding the law had taken place: 'Law, it might be argued, was coming to replace religion as the ideological cement which held society together.' The only real problem with this, with the Tudors in mind, and also the Stuart battles with parliament, was that arrest could be sudden, swift and without explanation.

One study of the blockhouses of Hull, which were fortress/prisons, is concerned with the imprisonment of Catholic recusants in Tudor times, and the author describes the kinds of arrest in that context, and to the 'priest hunters' of the time:

> *'After passing Acts involving heavy penalties it only remained for the Government to find willing officials to carry the law into effect. Twenty pounds were offered, under a Royal Proclamation, and one hundred pounds for the arrest of a Jesuit...Such tempting offers as these induced persons of both sexes to engage themselves in the role of priest-hunters.'*

But generally, (if we omit the excesses and tyrannies of the Tudor rulers), the monarch and the King's Bench, along with the other prerogative courts in the provinces, had the power to issue writs available to regulate the system and to try to countermand actions to detain given out in any one of the other courts in the land. The writ being issued meant that the official in question would have a warrant to arrest. The writ conferred a right or authority, and the authority to arrest a specified person is at the core of the present discussion.

An explanation of the writs issued and used is useful here, but the second section of this book, dealing with detention, will show more meticulously the use and power of the most relevant writs in the present context.

Habeas corpus 'You are to have the body'
This is the potent and prestigious writ at the very heart of the process of arrest and detention in English law. The full definition is *habeas corpus ad subjiciendum*, which is issued in order to bring a person out of an illegal detention or imprisonment. The King's Bench would issue this, having learned of an alleged arrest and confinement which is considered to be illegal. Obviously, a very common use of this writ was to remedy a situation which had been caused by a corrupt official; it dealt with abuse of power, and such abuses were easy to achieve when we consider the number of courts, petty officials, and also when one reflects on the vulnerability of the English class hierarchy to such actions as personal vendetta, malice, official preferment and removal of opposition.

Abuses of arrest were clearly most common and most problematic in times of national crisis and emergency.

Quo warranto 'with this power'
When first conceived, this was concerned with abuses of a royal franchise; since 1925 such proceedings against franchise infringement are civil. The writ itself is now no longer in existence.

Prerogative writs

These were issued for special, identified causes, in which the powerful weight of the Crown was moved to help and act for a wronged party. The crucial point here is that all subjects of the sovereign are to be aided by such writs when abuses happen and pleas are made. In reading crime history, particularly in accounts of court process, these writs will be referred to and discussed:

Procedendo 'proceeding'

If and when the judge in an inferior court (such as quarter sessions or family courts) caused a delay in judgement, he was ordered by this writ to get moving and make a decision.

Certiorari 'to be made certain'

This very commonly met in reading crime or legal history; the reason for this is that a cause which had been passed on from, say, a quarter session to an assize, was reverted to the first court. This would happen if at the first hearing there was a lack of substance in an area of the trial process.

Mandamus 'We command'

This is a strong command from the sovereign, and may be directed at individuals or inferior court, and relates to, in the words of Mozley's Dictionary of Law: 'directing them to do some particular thing which appertains to their office and duty...'

Case Studies

Hue and Cry and the Posse
Daniel Defoe and the Messengers 1693
General Warrants and John Wilkes 1763
Samuel Bamford 1817

These case studies from the past illustrate the complex interplay of individual freedom and the pragmatism of government; through the eyes of each establishment, potential radicals and dissidents, while protected by the rights of their being legal entities in the state, are enemies of peace and order.

Hue and Cry and the Posse

In that long period before the later Normans had begun to structure the courts and the regulation of processes in criminal law, who made arrests? The sheriffs (shire-reeves) and the constables for watch and ward could be involved, but the most common arrest might result from the hue and cry and the *posse commitatus*. The former was a general call for the pursuit of a wrong-doer. Proclamations were made openly 'in all counties, markets, hundreds, fairs and all other places where great resort of people is...'

The result was the formation of the posse, a word known perhaps most often from western novels and films. It was always the tradition, back in Anglo-Saxon society, for a man to have a weapon and to be ready to join such a posse. As in the westerns, he would be expected to respond to a sheriff if asked for help, and it was looked upon as his duty to act against the King's enemies and to do his part in hunting down a felon.

This raises the topic of outlawry. If a transgressor was named an outlaw he was seen as being exempt from the law's protection. He was exempt. He was a felon, and so he owned nothing, because all his possessions became Crown property; he could be pursued and seized of course, and he would find it very difficult to survive beyond civilised settlement. In spite of the legends of Robin Hood, the status of outlaw was likely to lead to a quick death, either from pursuers out hunting for vengeance, or by sheer vulnerability to exposure, disease, and attack from other rogues and bandits on the road.

A detained man who ran for freedom into the wilds could be labelled an outlaw if he had not responded to four court appeals or orders, and in fact he could be killed rather than merely arrested, by anyone acting in a posse. The notion of an outlaw was not abolished until 1879.

Daniel Defoe 1693 and the Messengers

Daniel Defoe knew many prisons. He knew them as a debtor as well as in the capacity of serious offender. He may be reckoned by many to be the father of the English novel, but in his life, his fiction was only one small part of the activities of this constantly busy, enterprising man. He is elusive: biographers often tackle the most elusive subjects; writers, artists and poets often spend so much time on their work that the business of biography is concerned with little else, but in Defoe's case, we have a man who was constantly involved in debate and interplay with the world he knew. That world was the late Stuart and early Georgian Britain, and in that age of chaotic social change when men were apt to rise and fall with equal rapidity, he was in his element. Why did he know prison? He experienced the inside of cells and sponging houses because his business brain and his writing expertise led him into trouble as often as it led him to success.

Before becoming a guest of Her Majesty Queen Anne in Newgate, Defoe knew the inside of a prison as a debtor. In the 1690's he was a married man, with a family, working as an entrepreneur in London and elsewhere; he was living at a time when 'projecting' was a way of life for many – those who dreamed of a major investment paying off and settling them in comfort for the rest of their lives. By that time, he was already a veteran of war, having fought for the wrong side in the Monmouth Rebellion of 1685, and his mind was bubbling with plans and ideas as he ventured into both authorship and business. Like many men of his time, he gathered creditors and gradually immersed himself in the murky waters of debt. He tried to fight off disaster by paying small amounts to ward off long-standing creditors, and then invest somewhere else, making major investments. This attitude to business ruined him. The turning point came when he decided to buy some civet cats, as the perfume from their gland secretions was valuable and the market for it was expanding. But he failed in the practicalities of it; even worse, he then invested money belonging to his mother-in-law and lost both affection and trust on his own doorstep. Matters began to involve the law; a man called Timothy Bird claimed an unpaid debt of £33 (promised to be paid within three months) and Defoe did not deliver. That was a huge sum in 1692.

Defoe had also invested at the same time in a diving bell business, and that too failed. He was then in deep trouble, as he was served with a subpoena and then, after failing to appear in court, with a commission of rebellion: that meant that should he not go to court, he was an outlaw and the officers were out to grab him. By November, 1693 he was in the King's Bench prison, awaiting trial. The situation for bankrupts at that time was horrendously grim: they could languish in prison until debts were sorted out and arrangements made. The amount he owed was a huge amount: a debt of £17,000 – in modern terms that would be around half a million pounds.

By the seventeenth century the gaols and bridewells (houses of correction) across the land had become places where all kinds of people were crammed together beyond society and left to rot. Only the wealthy, fallen foul of debtors, could enjoy a reasonably comfortable life behind the prison walls, because they could buy food and drink from the traders who came into the prisons. Generally, dumped into gaols were felons, debtors, small-time thieves, prostitutes, beggars and invalids. They were the last residence of what the society considered to be trash.

On 2 January, 1752 an anonymous prisoner wrote this letter to the *Gentleman's Magazine*:

Mr Urban,

I am an unhappy prisoner now lying in one of the gaols within this kingdom, to which I was committed about 10 months past, on an accusation of felony, though entirely innocent as afterwards appeared on my trial, my poverty and want of friends preventing any person till then from speaking the truth in my favour.

But the grievance I complain of is not my commitment for a crime of which I was not guilty, but the tyranny and oppression of the gaoler, for after I had been declared innocent by the jury, and the prosecution found to be on malice and ill-nature, instead of being immediately discharged, I was hurried back to the prison again, there to lie till I could raise 30s to pay the gaoler what he calls his fees. If any situation on earth merits pity or any evil merits the attention of the legislature, surely 'tis the case of unhappy prisoners in my circumstances. I have lain here six months, my family starving, my credit and character ruined and my spirits broken, without any means of procuring redress against the unjust prosecutor or any satisfaction for the numerous calamities he has brought upon me.

I have heard much talk of the equity of our laws but surely if they had not been defective or abused, I should not now suffer.'

The wretched man, in modern terms, had been on remand, guilty of no crime, and yet had been totally ruined in every aspect of his life and health. What we think of as 'remand' at that time was awaiting gaol delivery if at assizes, or some other kind of trial in other courts, and there were dozens of different courts across the land in the Georgian period, from manorial to admiralty and from military to assizes.

Defoe would be in a similar situation: stuck in a limbo among other debtors, at the mercy of his creditors, and of the gaoler, who wanted his own payment – the 'garnish' to do the minimum for his wretched charges. People visited the prisons, and they could gawp in sick fascination at the poor prisoners inside. The Clink, which has given its name as a general term for prison in English slang, was a short walk from London Bridge, and had existed since it started out as a part of the palace of the Bishop of Winchester, a man whose power would have extended to legal matters as well as religious; the land at Southwark was within the see of Winchester. The place was attacked by the Kentish rebels in1381, and later it became the main prison for religious offences, then, after the Great Fire, the City took control and sheriffs were given the power to deal with debtors, hence the use of the place for men like Defoe. It was destined to be burnt to the ground during the Gordon Riots of 1780 and it was never rebuilt.

All Defoe could do to extricate himself was to become the slave of his creditors; he agreed some terms with them and was released, but he still needed help, and luckily that came, in the person of Thomas Neale, who saw in Defoe a kindred spirit, a man who liked risk and enterprise, someone who was happy to try something innovative. The result was involvement in a lottery. Defoe was one of Neale's managers in a scheme which related to profit from ticket sales of course; his managers received a cut of that profit. Once again, Defoe was up and running, projecting, and taking risks. But he had experienced the highs and the lows of business life in Hanoverian Britain.

Of course he was also a man with an itch to write, and he loved writing polemics, stirring up debate, like a good journalist. In 1703 that got him into trouble again, this time with a publication called *The Shortest Way with the Dissenters*. He had foolishly written this with extreme irony, as Swift later did with his writing on the problem of homeless children; in Defoe's case, he wrote in the persona of a Whig expressing extreme views regarding the non-conformists. Defoe himself was brought up a dissenter of course, and he was using irony to show up some prominent aspects of worship which were hypocritical, such as occasional conformity, by which Anglicans in public office could maintain their worship as dissenters also. This all stemmed from his aim to show how intractable the established church was in its doctrines, and he underestimated the extent to which his writing would give offence. The Queen herself was moved to act, and Defoe was soon a wanted man.

He was on the run for some time, until finally arrested

on May 21, 1703 at a house in Spitalfields; two messengers grabbed him and he was interrogated before being taken to Newgate. An informer had been involved, receiving £50 for his work. Defoe was in Newgate for almost six months, and we have his own description of the impact of the place, as put into the mouth of his character Moll Flanders, in his novel of that name:

> I was now fixed indeed; 'tis impossible to describe the terror of my mind, when I was first brought in, and when I looked around upon all the horrors of that dismal place I looked upon myself as lost, and that I had nothing to think of, but of going out to the world, and that with the utmost infamy; the hellish noise, the roaring, swearing and clamour, the stench and nastiness, and all the dreadful crowd of afflicted things that I saw there, joined together to make the place seem an emblem of Hell itself, and an entrance into it.'

Notice here that he was arrested by 'messengers.' There was no police force in 1693.

Some of the most compelling historical stories come from the footnotes: the intriguing little small-print sentence at the bottom of the page that invites some further enquiry. When that note is combined with something puzzling and entirely new to the writer, then something opens out – an invitation to dig a little more deeply into the archives perhaps. That is exactly what happened when the idea for this book began. I have written widely in criminal history, and in the course of researching material for *Criminal River*, a history of the Thames River Police, I came across a paragraph recording an arrest made by 'two of the King's Messengers.' In 1810 two Messengers had arrested a man suspected of committing treason. They were not police officers.

In the course of dredging the archives of law and order in Regency England, when the River Police were being formed, I tended to encounter glimpses of these puzzling officers, in such snippets as these:

'On Friday, between six and seven o'clock, Mr Staley, a King's Messenger, was stopped by a single highwayman between Butcher's Grove and Granford bridge on the Hounslow Road, but on presenting a blunderbuss the highwayman rode off. As he was going out of the road his horse stumbled and threw him, upon which the post-boy pursued him...

'Mr Ellys, one of the King's oldest Messengers, on his return home from Minto, the seat of Sir Gilbert Elliot, had nearly lost his life by the carelessness of the driver; the chaise overturned and dragged but by the presence of mind of the old gentleman, he received only a few bruises.

'Sunday night Mr Flint, one of the King's Messengers, arrived at the Duke of Leeds's office with dispatches from Mr Whitworth, His Majesty's Minister at the court of Petersburg. He was also charged with dispatches from Mr Ewart, the British Minister at Berlin..'

Who were these men, who in 1810, when there was no national police force, made an arrest in London? They were not Bow Street Runners, that elite force stemming from Henry and John Fielding's mid-eighteenth century police court and network of thief-catchers. They were not military personnel. In an age in which proper professional police forces were being discussed and theorized, here were some men who were acting as officers with a power of arrest.

The year was important. In 1810, the paranoia created here in Britain by events across the Channel was at its height. In 1799–1800 the Combination Acts had been passed, and these made it clear that fear was in the streets; gatherings of more than a few folk on street corners were seditious; printers, writers and journalists were likely to be prosecuted and tried sometimes without a trial being guilty *in absentia* as the writ of Habeas Corpus was suspended. Only a year after these strange arrests, the Luddite violence was to erupt in Yorkshire, as machine-wreckers set to work on mills; the Bow Street Runners had been sent up to Huddersfield to help investigate workers' militancy. The special constables were called out. The militia were cleaning their guns.

In the midst of this, two King's Messengers made an arrest. I investigated the case a little, and sure enough, they were part of a very well-established corps of special government officials, and among other things, they had powers of arrest. But as their job title implies, they were essentially people who carried messages for the sovereign, and indeed that is what they are today, though much reduced in number.

But the sense of these men being engaged in something highly dangerous was increased when I learned that they are individuals who work alone, trusted with diplomatic baggage, and who travel almost anywhere. Today of course, there will be many technological developments that make the work more manageable and less risky, but I imagined a man in, say, 1850 travelling by rail from London to Turkey, with a briefcase strapped to his arm, with no military escort. He was the James Bond of Victoria's state.

General Warrants and John Wilkes 1763

A general warrant is a very powerful legal weapon if someone wants to resolve a problem by ignoring morality, basic rights, and humanitarian actions. In other words, back in the day, issuing a general warrant to have someone arrested was extreme, pragmatic and very effective – if there were no checks and restraints. The case of M.P. and radical John Wilkes, in the 1760s, shows the workings of general warrants.

Lord Denning, writing about the case, gives a succinct explanation of such documents:

> *'These warrants authorised the officers of the Crown to search premises for Libellous papers, to arrest the authors and publishers thereof, and to bring them before the Minister. All this was done without any previous notification or charge at all.'*

John Wilkes ran a periodical called *The North Briton*, which existed to be critical of the government; Wilkes, a friend of Dr Johnson and a man, though physically unattractive, had rare skills as a speaker and a very fine intellect. Lord Denning calls him 'a profligate demagogue.' He made enemies.

Opposed to him was Lord Camden (Sir Charles Pratt) and Camden was Lord Chief Justice of the Common Pleas. Sir Joshua Reynolds painted his portrait. In certain quarters of the London scene, Wilkes was popular, and the readership of the North Briton was considerable; but when it came to something in issue number 45 there was big trouble stirring for its editor. The provocation to the establishment and indeed to the king himself, was this in which he refers to the ruling party and to the king: 'They have sent the spirit of discord through the land, and I will prophesy that it will never be extinguished, but by the extinction of their power...I lament to see it sunk even to prostitution...'

This was interpreted as a seditious libel and the king himself, George III, was furious. A general warrant was issued against whoever produced that issue of the periodical – nobody was named specifically. The warrant was handed to the King's Messengers, whom we have already met with regard to Defoe. On 27 April, the Messengers started to make arrests. This included the printers involved as well as writers and of course the editor himself. A man called Huckle was arrested and handled with some civility, but when it came to John Wilkes, he was arrested at home in Westminster and all possessions of his in the home which might have been linked to the periodical were seized, and Wilkes was carted away.

But this action was known and Wilkes had friends. One of them – Serjeant Glynn, told Camden's court about the general warrant. Camden's response was, 'This is a most extraordinary warrant. Let an habeas corpus be issued immediately, returnable forthwith.'

What was the response of the men holding Wilkes? It was to lock him in the Tower of London. Something then happened which was always a thorn in the flesh of those wishing to right wrongs and cancel abusive and morally reprehensible documents such as that writ. Those holding Wilkes managed to get a warrant from the Secretary of State. Now, this is known as *mesne process*. This is the use of a warrant issued while a primary writ (habeas corpus here) is working. This meant that Wilkes was locked in the Tower and nobody was allowed to see him. There would have been an attachment to the counter-order from Camden's court, ordering Wilkes' release.

The response of the Messengers to the attachment was a bluff. They argued that they saw the order too late to act at the Tower. Glynn, who was fighting for Wilkes's cause, had a second habeas corpus issued. In court at last, it was asserted that through parliamentary privilege, Wilkes was free from arrest, and the charge of libel was not a felony or treasonable behaviour. Wilkes was eventually given the award of £1,000.

In 1766, just after these events, parliament made a Commons resolution:

> 'A motion was made... that a General Warrant for seizing and apprehending any person or persons being illegal, is, if executed upon a Member of this House, a breach of the privilege of this House.' Samuel Bamford 1817

During the years of panic and paranoia as events in Revolutionary France and the Napoleonic conquests put fear in the daily routine of the Britons, the radicals from the working classes presented an additional problem for the establishment. Their disorders, riots and seditious clubs and societies led some to believe that they might lead a revolution here too, and English heads might roll. Samuel Bamford was one such radical. He called his autobiography *Passages in the Life of a Radical*, and the book covers the years 1816 to 1821.

The account of his arrest in 1817 has a very modern ring to students of various societies across the world in 2020 where civil rights are ignored, and in fact, this account is no different from arrests by Hitler's Gestapo:

'I beheld Joseph Scott, deputy-constable of Middleton, hastening towards me. I concluded instantly that he wanted me; and disdaining the thought of flying, I returned and met him, and he took hold of me, saying I was a King's prisoner.

I asked him what for? And he said I should see presently; and we had not gone very far when we were met by Mr Nadin, deputy-constable of Manchester, and about six police officers, all well armed with staves, pistols and blunderbusses:

Two of these took hold of me, and the whole party marched back to the doctor's house. Here they handcuffed me... my wife in great distress rushed into the room. One Of the men had threatened to shoot her at the door....'

He was taken in a carriage, and another suspect was collected, and then eventually both were thrown in a cell. Bamford had still not been told what he was charged with.

There had been extreme measures against sedition and treason for quite some time. Habeas Corpus was suspended in1794 and this happened again just before Bamford was arrested. A number of Acts were passed to try to suppress 'seditious libel' and there were several trials for treason. In 1819 came the notorious Peterloo Massacre in Manchester, at which peaceful gathering the hussars were sent in with sabres flashing, to murder ordinary people who were there simply to listen to a speech by the radical, Henry Hunt.

From Victorian to Modern

With the creation of a professional police force, from 1829 on, the notion of an arrest began to become more tightly defined and described. Before that, of course there were arrests being made somewhere in the realm every day. These actions were taken by constables, magistrates, or other forces of law, such as the King's Messengers who have figured in the foregoing case studies. Since the 1780s there had been pockets of policing done, such as the Bow Street office in London, then the establishment of the Thames River Police at the end of the 1790s. There had also been the famous Bow Street Runners, and even a mounted force which patrolled around London intermittently. But for all those years before the actual national force, if an individual wished to prosecute someone, then justices – magistrates – and constables were the first stage in that process.

Many of the arrests made within these processes were dependant on local knowledge and on custom, as well as on the basic social relationships that maintain order. Clive Emsley, in his history of British police, has a representative example of this: 'In 1636 ... John King, an Essex villager, stole eight hens. He was quickly apprehended by Thomas Burrowes, the local constable. King begged not to be prosecuted, stressing that it was his first offence; after a long talk with the victim of the offence, Burrowes resolved to release King...'

A normal process was for a crime to be reported when it had been determined or alleged, and the accusers would go to the local magistrate and complete a declaration. A very good instance of this is the following from Beverley in Yorkshire at the end of the eighteenth century. The heart of a following arrest was this *recognizance.*

This story is about how a simple cluster of recognisances may open up a tale of sensational high drama – and it involves several local families around a village in East Yorkshire. It is a perfect illustration of how documents from the past may open up into whole areas of fascination in the broader narrative of the age.

To establish first of all exactly what a recognisance is: this is a bond, acknowledged in front of a justice or similar officer, the aim being to 'secure an action by the person named in the document.' In other words, lots of people around the village in question saw cruelty going on before them and they went to see the magistrate. Once they had filled in a recognisance, they were committed to play a part in a prosecution.

Beverley, the Yorkshire market town, was trying to keep up with its grand neighbour, York, in the eighteenth century. It felt that it had a dash of culture and gentry. In fact, throughout the eighteenth century, the planning and architectural developments had been impressive. The rebuilding of the town hall came in 1762, and the courthouse and other municipal buildings were to enhance the appearance of this attractive place of social meetings, hostelries, and visitors on their way to the coast. But beneath this lay the usual dark problems and violence of the Georgian years. In fact, it was the setting for a brutal killing of a defenceless little child.

In the last year of the eighteenth century, when the so-called Age of Reason was flowering, the East Riding Assizes were to witness one of the most repulsive and inhuman cases the annals of murder have ever recorded. It happened at the village of Long Riston, a place described in the nineteenth century as, '*... standing on the high road from Hull to Bridlington, eleven miles from the former place and nineteen from the latter... There are chapels in the village belonging to the primitive and Wesleyan Methodists erected in 1836. The National School was built by subscription for the accommodation of 100* Children... It is endowed with about £12 per annum, left by Peter *Nevill in 1807.*'

Around the turn of the century then, just as religion and local philanthropy were having an effect, there was one little boy who would not be attending that new national school: that was Thomas Hostler.

At the midsummer assizes for 1799 the true nature of the cruel death of little Thomas was recorded for posterity in the careful and ornate longhand of 'B. Ford.' What happened was that the boy's father, William, together with his wife Jane and his sister-in-law, Elisabeth Beal, who had been maltreating little Thomas went too far. Neighbours could take it no more: they had witnessed extreme cruelty and this had been happening over a long period. Finally, they acted.

Four people of the village took out a recognizance against the three abusers, and at that time the child was not dead. Christopher Hall, Elisabeth Chadwell, Sarah Wray and Mary Ford stated upon oath that the three defendants had physically abused the little boy, most intensively over a period of several weeks in June of that year. That document meant that each of the accusers was bound to pay thirty pounds to his majesty George III if the action failed. There was going to be little chance of that ever happening. What had been done to the boy was savage beyond belief.

Going so far as to take out a recognizance was a serious

commitment. The wording on the paper, under which the person had to sign, was:

'The condition of this recognizance is such, that if the above shall personally appear at the next general quarter sessions of this Peace, to be holden in the said Riding and there testify and give evidence on behalf of our Sovereign Lord the King, then his voice shall be heard by the learned magistrate...'

If not, then the person would have to pay a few shillings in a fine. If an ordinary citizen went so far as to sign that statement, then they were serious about their charge. The case here went to the court and there were arrests, charges and convictions.

In the Victorian period, as the police expanded and regional constabularies were gradually formed, the statutes governing police actions and responsibilities make it clear that it took a long time for arrests to become smoothly carried out. There were all kinds of anomalies and contradictions. A swift survey of short reports on arrests through the nineteenth century soon brings such items as this into focus:

'Mr Cecil Chapman at the Tower Bridge Police Court, London, on Tuesday, referring to a man charged with theft, who had been kept in custody since his arrest on Monday at noon awaiting the return of an alleged stolen property from Swindon, said the man should have been brought into court on Monday. As quickly as possible after arrest a man should be tried for the offence with which he was charged.'

The new police found themselves faced with a stream of

odd, complex, intractable situations, reported by the public or dealt with by an officer on the beat; these matters all needed relating to the law as it filtered down into police handbooks. The expanding police courts, which took much of the work of magistrates' courts as the Victorian years went on, were faced with a proliferation of offences relating mostly to poverty, deprivation, drunkenness and social pressures such as unemployment, industrial injury and mental illness.

Some cases are bizarre, such as when a couple returning home late at night saw a man defecating outside their house. They went in search of a constable. What ensued was a scenario seen every day by the new police: infringements and petty theft in which there was no witness and everything hinged on who saw what and how reliable (or verified) was the view of the alleged crime?

With the twentieth century came the more sophisticated, streamlined work of the police officer, and along came the manuals, handbooks, guides and legal abstracts. In 1920, Stanley Sevill wrote *The Police Service of England and Wales*, and it was published by John Kempster of the Police Review, which was a professional journal especially for the police officer, covering all important aspects of his or her work. This volume has fifteen pages of small print devoted to the notion of arrest, and statutory powers and edicts are linked to every police action taken. This work deals admirably with the actual nature of an arrest, with all its complexities created by the human situation:

'An offender may be brought before Justices by summons, based upon verbal or written information laid before them and when the only consideration is to bring the offender before a tribunal within a reasonable time, the police

should resort to a summons...But even when there is no suggestion of the offender absconding, or no fear of his escape, it may be necessary in the public interest that he should be removed from the community...'

By 1938, when the Home Office published its report on detective work, the difficult topic of arrest without warrant in certain cases could be handled more succinctly. The basis had always been that the distinction between a felony and a misdemeanour was the deciding factor, a misdemeanour being an offence without the concomitant penalty of losing property and land, which defined a felony. (The distinction was abolished in 1967). But the report admitted that the distinctions between the two are sometimes 'artificial' and could be anomalous. The stipulations in law at the time between who could or could not be arrested without a warrant were a headache for the officer at work:

'The offences of obtaining credit by fraud or by a false pretence, for instance, are misdemeanours, and there is no general power to arrest without warrant a person suspected of committing them (unless he is found committing them at night).

In such manner is the tricky business of arrest and detention dealt with. The way this is expressed is very perfunctory, but every legal official knows the massive gap between the law as a written text and the law in action, when dealing with people.

By the Edwardian period and during the First World War, there were, of course 'extraordinary powers' and there was always the DORA (Defence of the Realm Act) behind police work. This was passed in 1914, and the immediate context was the nature of espionage organised by Germany, and the establishment in Britain of MI5. As with previous wars and international threats to public security, the nature of arrest became rather more flexible.

Contemporary: Stuart Gibbon

During this section I'm going to explain the powers and procedures associated with an arrest, with the addition of case law, case studies and practical examples for context. The actual process of making an arrest hasn't changed immeasurably over the last few decades but, as you will see, the powers and conditions which ensure that an arrest is lawful have evolved over time. Let's start by taking a look at one of our fundamental rights and freedoms and how it may be restricted in certain circumstances.

Human Rights

The arrest of a person deprives them of their liberty and security and, as such, engages Article 5 of the European Convention on Human Rights. There are a number of lawful reasons why someone may be deprived of their freedom.

Article 5 of the Convention states:
1. Everyone has the right to liberty and security of person. No one shall be deprived of his liberty save in the following cases and in accordance with a procedure prescribed by law:
(a) the lawful detention of a person after conviction by a competent court
(b) the lawful arrest or detention of a person for non-compliance with the lawful order of a court or in order

to secure the fulfilment of any obligation prescribed by law

(c) the lawful arrest or detention of a person effected for the purpose of bringing him before the competent legal authority on reasonable suspicion of having committed an offence or when it is reasonably considered necessary to prevent his committing an offence or fleeing after having done so

(d) the detention of a minor by lawful order for the purpose of educational supervision or his lawful detention for the purpose of bringing him before the competent legal authority

(e) the lawful detention of persons for the prevention of the spreading of infectious diseases, of persons of unsound mind, alcoholics or drug addicts or vagrants

(f) the lawful arrest or detention of a person to prevent his effecting an unauthorised entry into the country or of a person against whom action is being taken with a view to deportation or extradition

Article 5 ECHR doesn't provide any power to arrest or detain a person but documents the circumstances where our general right to liberty may be interfered with by lawful means. A person can only be deprived of their general right to liberty under one or more of the above conditions which must be carried out in accordance with a procedure prescribed by law. The most common condition where Article 5 is engaged by the police is probably Article 5(1)(c) where there is reasonable suspicion that a person has committed an offence or to prevent them committing an offence or making off afterwards.

In addition to the above conditions, Article 5 goes on to state:

2. Everyone who is arrested shall be informed promptly, in a language which he understands, of the reasons for his arrest and of any charge against him.

3. Everyone arrested or detained in accordance with the provisions of paragraph 1(c) of this Article shall be brought promptly before a judge or other officer authorised by law to exercise judicial power and shall be entitled to trial within a reasonable time or to release pending trial. Release may be conditioned by guarantees to appear for trial.

4. Everyone who is deprived of his liberty by arrest or detention shall be entitled to take proceedings by which the lawfulness of his detention shall be decided speedily by a court and his release ordered if the detention is not lawful.

5. Everyone who has been the victim of arrest or detention in contravention of the provisions of this Article shall have an enforceable right to compensation.

The right to be told the reasons for arrest, in a language which can be understood, allows for the arrested person to be able to challenge the lawfulness of the arrest and detention where appropriate.

Powers of arrest

The police will usually resort to arrest in relation to the commission of an alleged offence, but sometimes an arrest may be made to stop something from happening. An example would be where a person is arrested in order to prevent a breach of the peace but is subsequently released when there is no further likelihood of that breach re-occurring. An arrest may also be made in order to bring someone before a court, to take samples or fingerprints, or to return someone to prison. A police power to arrest someone may come from the conditions at the time (allowing an arrest under Section 24 of the Police and Criminal Evidence Act 1984), the provisions of a particular Act (Section 7 of the Bail Act 1976 – absconding from bail), the provisions of an order (a court order or a warrant) or common law (breach of the peace).

Information to be given on arrest

When someone is arrested, regardless of the legal power being used or the reason for arrest, Section 28 of the Police and Criminal Evidence Act 1984 (often simply referred to as PACE) clearly documents the information that must be given to a person upon arrest.

Section 28 Police and Criminal Evidence Act 1984

(1) Subject to subsection (5) below, where a person is arrested, otherwise than by being informed that he is under arrest, the arrest is not lawful unless the person arrested is informed that he is under arrest as soon as is practicable after his arrest.

(2) Where a person is arrested by a constable, subsection (1) above applies regardless of whether the fact of the arrest is obvious.

(3) Subject to subsection (5) below, no arrest is lawful unless the person arrested is informed of the grounds for the arrest at the time of, or as soon as is practicable after, the arrest.

(4) Where a person is arrested by a constable, subsection (3) above applies regardless of whether the grounds for the arrest are obvious.

(5) Nothing in this section is to be taken to require a person to be informed –

(a) that he is under arrest; or

(b) of the grounds for the arrest,

if it was not reasonably practicable for him to be so informed by reason of his having escaped from arrest before the information could be given.

Put simply, the arresting officer has to tell the person that he is under arrest and give them the grounds for the arrest unless the person runs off before the officer has the opportunity to tell them. The person must still be given this information as and when they are captured. The arrest would be considered unlawful if the information is not given.

There have been cases which have been subject to appeal on the basis that the actual word 'arrest' hadn't been used by the officer at the time, but there is nothing in the provisions to confirm the actual wording which should be used, nor exactly when. Phrases such as "you're nicked" have been considered acceptable as long as the person understands its meaning.

CASE LAW – (R v Fiak 2005)

Fiak had been sitting in a car, parked outside his house, when he was approached by police officers who suspected that he was in control of the vehicle having consumed too much alcohol. He denied driving the vehicle and claimed that he had left the house following an argument with his wife. The police detained Fiak while they questioned his wife about what had happened. Fiak ignored this and a struggle broke out between him and an officer, who claimed she had been injured. He was restrained and taken to the police station. Fiak claimed that until the word 'arrest' had actually been spoken, there had been no lawful arrest and restraining him was not appropriate. He appealed to the courts but this was dismissed with the finding that the police officer's conduct had been appropriate in detaining him. The officer did not use the word 'arrest' until the investigation was concluded, at which point the grounds existed to lawfully make the arrest.

Use of handcuffs on arrest

The police are entitled to use 'reasonable force' when effecting an arrest. Legal powers to use such force are derived from various sources of legislation including Section 3(1) Criminal Law Act 1967 and Section 117 of the PACE Act 1984. Any use of force must be lawful, proportionate and necessary in the circumstances. The use of handcuffs to restrain an arrested person should be an objective decision made on an individual basis and capable of scrutiny. In other words, not every person who has been arrested needs to be handcuffed. If they have been or are likely to become violent or may try to escape then the application of handcuffs is perfectly justified. If however, they are compliant and appear to pose no risk to the officers or wider public then there may be no need to handcuff them. If the situation were to escalate then the decision may need to be reviewed. If you're writing an arrest scene it's worth bearing this in mind.

The police caution

Warnings against people incriminating themselves have existed since the beginning of the twentieth century, possibly earlier. In 1912 the judges of the King's Bench issued the Judges' Rules which provided that, when the police had admissible evidence to suspect a person of an offence and wished to question that suspect about the offence, the officer should first caution the person that he was entitled to remain silent. In R v Leckey (1943) the Court of Criminal Appeal commented in relation to self-incrimination with the words ... 'an innocent person might well, either from excessive caution or for some other reason, decline to say anything when charged and cautioned, and if it were possible to hold that out to a jury as a ground on which they might find a man guilty, it is obvious that innocent persons might be in great peril'. It was around this time that a caution was established using the following words – You have the right to remain silent, but anything you do say will be taken down and may be used in evidence.

The introduction of the Police and Criminal Evidence Act 1984 saw major reform to the questioning and treatment of suspected offenders. The wording of the caution was confirmed as – You do not have to say anything unless you wish to do so but what you say may be given in evidence.

As a result of the introduction of the Criminal Justice and Public Order Act 1994, the police caution was further amended to reflect the fact that people arrested were no longer able to remain silent without the potential that this course of action may prejudice their case. The caution, which is still used at time of publishing (2020) is – **You do not have to say anything, but it may harm your defence if you do not mention when questioned something which you later rely on in court. Anything you do say may be given in evidence**.

Put simply, you can still remain silent, but if you say something in court which you didn't mention when given the opportunity in a police interview, the court may consider why you didn't mention it to the police at the time, and could draw its own conclusions. This consideration is known as 'drawing an adverse inference'.

The Police and Criminal Evidence Act (PACE) Code of Practice, Code C requires that a person must be cautioned upon arrest or further arrest. Section 117 of PACE allows for the use of reasonable force when making an arrest, whether such force is 'reasonable' is a matter for the courts to determine, in the light of all the circumstances, including the circumstances as the arresting officer believed them to be at the time. Use of excessive force, while amounting to possible misconduct and assault, doesn't make an otherwise lawful arrest unlawful.

Arrest in Scotland

The Criminal Justice (Scotland) Act 2016 is the legislation which provides the guidance for the police in Scotland in relation to arrests. Where the suspected offence is not punishable by imprisonment, the police should only arrest if satisfied that it would not be in the interests of justice to delay the arrest. On arrest the police officer should read out the following statement;

- "I am arresting you under Section 1 of the Criminal Justice (Scotland) Act 2016
- for (state general nature of offence).
- The reason for your arrest is that I suspect that you have committed an offence and I believe that keeping you in custody is necessary and proportionate for the purposes of bringing you before a court or otherwise dealing with you in accordance with the law.
  Do you understand?
- You are not obliged to say anything but anything you do say will be noted and may be used in evidence.
  Do you understand? (note any reply).

- I require you to give me your name, date of birth, place of birth, nationality and address.
- You have the right to have a solicitor informed of your arrest; and to have access to a solicitor. These rights will be explained to you further at a police station."

The police in Scotland would usually progress less serious crimes, not punishable with imprisonment, by applying for a warrant to a Sheriff or Justice of the Peace.

PACE Code of Practice Code G

Code G of the Police and Criminal Evidence Act 1984 provides guidance for the statutory power of arrest by police officers and applies to any arrest made by a police officer after midnight on 12th November 2012. The Code covers a number of areas including discrimination and Human Rights. It also documents the legislation which gives police the authority to arrest as follows – 'Section 24 of the Police and Criminal Evidence Act 1984 (as substituted by section 110 of the Serious Organised Crime and Police Act 2005) provides the statutory power for a constable to arrest without warrant for all offences.' The Code of Practice must be readily available at all police stations for consultation by police officers and police staff, detained persons and members of the public. Although the Code provides the power to a constable, an arrest can be made by any police officer, regardless of rank.

Section 24 PACE Act 1984 (as amended by Section 110 Serious Organised Crime and Police Act 2005)
A lawful arrest requires two elements:
A person's involvement or suspected involvement or attempted involvement in the commission of a criminal offence AND

reasonable grounds for believing that the person's arrest is necessary. Both of these elements must be satisfied and communicated to the arrested person at the time.

(a) Involvement 'in the commission of an offence'
A constable may arrest without warrant in relation to any offence anyone:

- who is about to commit an offence or is in the act of committing an offence
- whom the officer has reasonable grounds for suspecting is about to commit an offence or to be committing an offence
- whom the officer has reasonable grounds to suspect of being guilty of an offence which he or she has reasonable grounds for suspecting has been committed
- anyone who is guilty of an offence which has been committed or anyone whom the officer has reasonable grounds for suspecting to be guilty of that offence

There must be some reasonable, objective grounds for the suspicion, based on known facts and information which are relevant to the likelihood that the offence has been committed and that the person liable to arrest committed it.

For the purposes of Code G, an 'offence' means any statutory or common law offence for which a person may be tried by a Magistrates' Court or the Crown Court and punished if convicted. The Code doesn't apply to powers of arrest conferred on constables under any arrest warrant (issued by a court), the Bail Act 1976, or to the powers of constables to arrest without warrant, other than under s. 24 of PACE for an offence. These other powers to arrest without warrant don't depend on the arrested person committing any specific offence and include powers under the Mental

Health Act 1983, the Road Traffic Act 1988, and common law.

Reasonable grounds to suspect

The concept of 'reasonable grounds for suspecting' has yet to be fully tested by the courts but does require an element of objectivity and whether, in the circumstances, a reasonable and sober person might have formed a similar view to that of the police officer.

The fact that a person may be in a small group, one of whom must have committed the offence, can amount to reasonable grounds for suspecting that person.

CASE LAW – (Cumming and others v Chief Constable of Northumbria Police 2003)
The five claimants, employees in a department concerned with monitoring recordings made by CCTV cameras, had been arrested following the discovery of tampering with tapes which showed the possible commission of an offence. On their claims for damages for wrongful arrest and false imprisonment, the Judge had found that the police had acted in good faith, had reasonable grounds for suspecting the claimants of committing an arrestable offence, and that the decision to arrest was a proper exercise of their discretion. The claimants appealed on the grounds that, since they had no links with the suspected offender, were all of good character and mere opportunity could not amount to a fact sufficient to found the reasonable suspicion required by Section 24(6) of the Police and Criminal Evidence Act 1984, the judge was wrong in both latter respects.

The claimants' appeal was dismissed with the court finding that there was nothing in principle either preventing opportunity from amounting to reasonable grounds for suspicion sufficient to entitle the police to make an arrest, or with arresting more than one person, even if the crime could only have been committed by one person. It was also found that, based on the evidence, the Judge had been entitled to accept that the police had taken all reasonable steps and had been left with the fact that one or more of those arrested must have been the culprit.

(b) Necessity criteria

The power of arrest is only exercisable if the constable has reasonable grounds for believing that it is necessary to arrest the person. The statutory criteria which document what may constitute 'necessity' are summarised below and are an operational decision at the discretion of the constable as to;

- which one or more of the necessity criteria (if any) applies to the individual; and
- if any of the criteria do apply, whether to arrest, grant street bail after arrest, report for summons or for charging by post, issue a fixed penalty notice or take any other action that is open to the officer

Extending the power of arrest to all offences provides a constable with the ability to use that power to deal with any situation. However, applying the necessary criteria requires the constable to examine and justify the reason or reasons why a person needs to be arrested or (as the case may be) further arrested for an offence.

When it is practicable to tell a person why their arrest is necessary, the constable should outline the facts, information and other circumstances which provide the grounds for believing that their arrest is necessary and which the officer considers satisfy one or more of the following statutory criteria:

(a) to enable the name of the person in question to be ascertained (in the case where the constable does not know and cannot readily ascertain, the persons name, or has reasonable grounds for doubting whether a name given by the person as his name is his real name):

An officer might decide that a persons name cannot be readily ascertained if they fail or refuse to give it when asked, particularly after being warned that failure or refusal is likely to make their arrest necessary. Where mobile fingerprinting is available and the suspects name cannot be ascertained or is doubted, the officer should consider using the power under Section 61(6A) of PACE to take and check the fingerprints of a suspect as this may avoid the need to arrest solely to enable their name to be ascertained.

(b) to enable the address of the person in question to be ascertained. Grounds to doubt an address given may arise if the person appears reluctant or hesitant when asked to give their address or is unable to provide verifiable details of the locality they claim to live in.

(c) to prevent the person in question –

    (i)   causing physical injury to himself or any other person – this might apply where the suspect has already used or threatened violence against others and it is thought likely that they may assault others if they are not arrested.

    (ii) suffering physical injury – this might apply where the suspects behaviour and actions are believed likely to provoke, or have provoked, others to want to assault the suspect unless the suspect is arrested for their own protection.

(iii) causing loss or damage to property – this might apply where the suspect is a known persistent offender with a history of serial offending against property (theft and criminal damage) and it is thought likely that they may continue offending if they are not arrested.

(iv) committing an offence against public decency (only applies where members of the public going about their normal business cannot reasonably be expected to avoid the person in question) – this might apply when an offence against public decency is being committed in a place to which the public have access and is likely to be repeated in that or some other public place at a time when the public are likely to encounter the suspect.

(v) causing an unlawful obstruction of the highway – this might apply to any offence where its commission causes an unlawful obstruction which it is believed may continue or be repeated if the person is not arrested, particularly if the person has been warned that they are causing an obstruction.

(d) to protect a child or other vulnerable person from the person in question – this might apply when the health (physical or mental) or welfare of a child or vulnerable person is likely to be harmed or is at risk of being harmed, if the person is not arrested, in cases where it is not practicable and appropriate to make alternative arrangements to prevent the suspect from having any harmful or potentially harmful contact with the child or vulnerable person.

(e) to allow the prompt and effective investigation of the offence or of the conduct of the person in question – this may arise when it is thought likely that unless the person is arrested and then either taken in custody to the police station or granted 'street bail' to attend the station later, further action considered necessary to properly investigate their involvement in the offence would be frustrated, unreasonably delayed or otherwise hindered and therefore be impracticable. Examples when this may apply include:

(i)   interviewing the suspect on occasions when the person's voluntary attendance is not considered to be a practicable alternative to arrest – this might apply if the person is unlikely to attend voluntarily, the person has made false statements and/or presented false evidence or it is thought likely that they may steal or destroy evidence, may collude or contact other suspects or may intimidate, threaten or contact witnesses. This list is not exhaustive but provides some examples for context.

(ii) when considering arrest in connection with the investigation of an indictable offence, there is a need:

- to enter and search without a search warrant any premises occupied or controlled by the arrested person or where the person was when arrested or immediately before arrest;
- to prevent the arrested person from having contact with others;
- to detain the arrested person for more than 24 hours before charge.

It should be remembered that certain powers available as the result of an arrest (eg entry and search of premises, detention without charge beyond 24 hours, holding a person incommunicado and delaying access to legal advice) only apply in respect of indictable offences (those triable at the Crown Court) and are subject to the specific requirements on authorisation as set out in PACE and the relevant Codes of Practice.

(iii) when considering arrest in connection with any recordable offence and it is necessary to secure or preserve evidence of that offence by taking fingerprints, footwear impressions or samples from the suspect for evidential comparison or matching with other material relating to that offence, for example, from the crime scene.

(iv) when considering arrest in connection with any offence and it is necessary to search, examine or photograph the person to obtain evidence.

The necessity criteria do not permit arrest solely to enable the routine taking, searching and retention of fingerprints, samples, footwear impressions and photographs when there are no prior grounds to believe that checking and comparing the fingerprints etc or taking a photograph would provide relevant evidence of the person's involvement in the offence concerned or would help to ascertain or verify his/her real identity.

(v) when considering arrest in connection with an offence to which the statutory Class A drug testing requirements in Code C section 17 apply, to enable testing when it is thought that drug misuse might have caused or contributed to the offence.

The meaning of 'prompt' at (e) should be considered on a case-by-case basis taking account of all the circumstances. It indicates that the progress of the investigation should not be delayed to the extent that it would adversely affect the effectiveness of the investigation. The arresting officer also has discretion to release the arrested person on 'street bail' as an alternative to taking the person directly to the police station.

(f) to prevent any prosecution for the offence from being hindered by the disappearance of the person in question – this may arise when it is thought that the person is unlikely to attend court if they are not arrested or the address given by the person is not a satisfactory address for service of a summons or a written charge.

Summary

I appreciate that there is an awful lot of information to take in about the arrest of a person so thought this would be a good point to provide a brief summary. In order for an arrest to be considered lawful, there must be reason to believe that the person has been involved in an offence and that it is necessary to arrest that person. There are a number of criteria which may justify the necessity to arrest. These include the need to ascertain the name or address of a person, to prevent injury or damage or to protect a child or vulnerable person. An additional criteria, which is probably the most frequently used, is 'to allow the prompt and effective investigation of the offence or of the conduct of the person in question'. This may apply if the police need to interview that person, search premises, take samples or use other powers conferred by the PACE Act 1984. An arrested person should be told that they are under arrest, given the grounds and reason for the arrest, and cautioned on arrest.

Arrest examples

1) PC Flynn receives a call from the force control room to attend a disturbance outside a shop. As she arrives in a marked police car she sees Rodgers lean into a nearby skip and remove something. He then throws the item at the window of the shop causing the glass to shatter. PC Flynn pulls up and approaches Flynn, who appears to have been drinking. PC Flynn says to Rodgers "You are under arrest for criminal damage as I've just seen you break that window. Your arrest is necessary for the prompt and effective investigation of the offence and to prevent you from causing further damage". The officer then cautions Flynn "You do not have to say anything but it may harm your defence if you do not mention when questioned something which you later rely on in court. Anything you do say may be given in evidence". In reply to the caution Flynn says "He wouldn't sell me any beer, that'll teach him". Due to his aggressive behaviour he is handcuffed and placed in the rear of the police car before being taken to the police station. A house brick is recovered from the pavement outside the shop.

2) PC Wilson is called to a supermarket where Hall has been detained by a security guard on suspicion of theft of a bottle of gin. Hall was seen to place the bottle inside his jacket and leave the store, making no attempt to pay for the item. He was stopped outside and invited back into the store. The bottle of gin was recovered and the police were called. On their arrival the security guard tells PC Wilson what happened in the presence and hearing of Hall. PC Wilson then cautions Hall "You do not have to say anything but it may harm your defence if you do not mention when questioned something which you later rely on in court.

Anything you do say may be given in evidence". The officer then says "You have heard what the security guard has said, is there anything you want to say?" Hall replies "I'm saying nothing, just charge me." Due to the circumstances and local force policy in relation to shop theft, PC Wilson may not need to resort to arrest and could look at alternative options to deal with the incident. He asks Hall for his name and address on several occasions but Hall refuses to provide any details. PC Wilson does not recognise Hall nor is there anything on his person which may help to identify him. Having exhausted this approach PC Wilson says to Hall "You are under arrest on suspicion of theft as you were seen leaving the store without paying for a bottle of gin which was hidden inside your jacket. Your arrest is necessary because you won't tell me your name and address and I don't know who you are". PC Wilson then reminds Hall that he is under caution and he is taken to the police station to be interviewed about the incident.

CASE STUDY – WRONGFUL ARREST

The Court of Appeal judgement in *Parker v Chief Constable of Essex* is of considerable significance in relation to the level of damages payable in cases of unlawful detention and the issue of 'reasonable grounds' to arrest a person.

The claim arose from a cold case investigation undertaken by Essex police into the death of Stuart Lubbock. Mr Lubbock was found unconscious in the swimming pool at the home of entertainer Michael Barrymore – real name Michael Parker – in 2001, and was later pronounced dead. Nobody was prosecuted at the time in relation to the death. Essex police commenced a full review of all available evidence in 2006. This led to the arrest of Mr Parker and two others in 2007 on suspicion of offences relating to the death.

Essex police chose to arrest all three suspects simultaneously, even though they were in different locations, to avoid collusion, and implemented a co-ordinated plan for the arrests. However, on the way to arrest Mr Parker the designated arresting officer, DC Jenkins, became stuck in traffic. The arrest could not be delayed so a decision was made for another police officer present at the scene, PC Cootes, to carry out the arrest. Mr Parker was arrested and questioned before being released. No charges were brought against him. He issued a claim for substantial damages for wrongful arrest and false imprisonment, alleging that the arrest had destroyed his career, which he had been successfully rebuilding, after the adverse publicity at the time of Mr Lubbock's death.

In English law, a police officer carrying out an arrest of a person, must personally have reasonable grounds to suspect the person of the offence(s) for which they are being arrested (known as the *'O'Hara* principle'). The designated arresting officer, DC Jenkins, was fully appraised of the facts of the case, and on the Chief Constable's submission, the evidence gathered provided ample grounds for the arrest. However, the actual arresting officer, PC Cootes, knew very little – Essex police had controlled the sharing of information on a 'need to know' basis. He therefore, under *O'Hara*, did not have reasonable grounds to arrest Mr Parker.

The Chief Constable conceded that the arrest was unlawful for breach of the *O'Hara* principle, but sought to rely upon what is known as the *'Lumba* principle'. This is derived from a Supreme Court case (2011) which held that, where a person had been unlawfully detained by the Home Secretary, due to a technical breach of procedure under the Immigration Act, that person should only be entitled to nominal damages if the person could have been lawfully detained in any event under other provisions. Therefore, the Chief Constable argued, the unlawful arrest by the police should be recognised by an award of nominal damages only, as Mr Parker would have been lawfully arrested if DC Jenkins had not been delayed in traffic.

At first instance, Mr Justice Stuart-Smith found that:

- Essex police as a corporate body did have reasonable grounds to suspect Mr Parker of the offences for which he was arrested, but the arresting police officer did not himself have sufficient grounds for the arrest in his mind, and
- *Lumba* did not apply to the circumstances of the case, and Mr Parker was therefore entitled to substantial damages.

The Chief Constable appealed to the Court of Appeal, on the issue of damages. Mr Parker cross appealed, arguing that Essex police as a corporate body did not have reasonable grounds to arrest him. Lord Justice Leveson gave the judgement of the Court of Appeal on behalf of all three Judges.

First, he found that Essex police did have reasonable grounds to suspect Mr Parker of the offences for which he was arrested. He then went on to hold that *Lumba* should be applied to this case. He set out the test to be used to determine whether nominal damages only should be awarded: what would have happened had Essex police appreciated what the law required them to do? Looking at the facts, if Essex police had realised that the arresting police officer needed to be personally apprised of the facts they would have organised for the arresting police officer to be briefed, probably by phone to the scene, by a senior officer. Therefore, Mr Parker was entitled to nominal damages only.

The test to be applied for determining whether nominal damages should be paid in a claim for wrongful arrest or false imprisonment, is clearly set out in the Court of Appeal's Judgement. It should be expected to apply not only to claims based on the *O'Hara* point, but also to a range of claims currently brought for breach of the provisions of the Police and Criminal Evidence Act 1984 (such as for failure to carry out a review of custody after the set periods, or a failure to provide correct information to an arrested person at the time of arrest).

This decision rebalances the law of false imprisonment, permitting those who have been subject to false imprisonment to obtain a legal declaration to that effect, but allowing only a nominal award for damages, where the person detained would still have been detained had the police officers appreciated at the time that they were making an error. It also recognises that the *O'Hara* principle does not sit easily with modern, complex and sensitive investigations, where not every potential arresting police officer can or should be fully briefed.

Record of arrest

The arresting officer is required to record in their pocket book or by other methods used for recording information:

- the nature and circumstances of the offence leading to the arrest
- the reason or reasons why arrest was necessary

- the fact that the caution was given
- anything said by the person at the time of the arrest

The record should be made at the time of arrest, unless impracticable, or as soon as possible afterwards. On arrival at the police station, or after being first arrested at the police station, the arrested person must be brought before the custody officer as soon as practicable and a custody record must be opened. The information given by the arresting officer about the circumstances and reason(s) for arrest shall be recorded as part of the custody record, which will serve as a record of the arrest.

Citizen's arrest

The Police and Criminal Evidence Act 1984 (PACE) makes provision for the so-called 'citizen's arrest'. Far narrower than the police powers, these powers of arrest are set out in Section 24A, which states:

(1) A person other than a constable may arrest without a warrant –
   (a) anyone who is in the act of committing an indictable offence;
   (b) anyone whom he has reasonable grounds for suspecting to be committing an indictable offence.
(2) Where an indictable offence has been committed, a person other than a constable may arrest without a warrant –
   (a) anyone who is guilty of the offence;
   (b) anyone whom he has reasonable grounds for suspecting to be guilty of it.
(3) But the power of summary arrest conferred by subsection (1) or (2) is exercisable only if
   (a) the person making the arrest has reasonable

grounds for believing that, for any of the reasons mentioned in subsection (4), it is necessary to arrest the person in question; and

(b) it appears to the person making the arrest that it is not reasonably practicable for a constable to make it instead.

(4) The reasons referred to in subsection (3)(a) are to prevent the person in question:

(a) causing physical injury to himself or any other person;

(b) suffering physical injury;

(c) causing loss of or damage to property; or

(d) making off before a constable can assume responsibility for him.

Unlike the powers of arrest available to police officers (which apply to any offence), the citizen's power of arrest only applies where the offence in question is indictable. An indictable offence is an offence which can be heard at the Crown Court and would usually be one of the more serious offences such as murder, rape, robbery or burglary. This power of arrest is available to police staff and others such as Police Community Support Officers (PCSO).

Citizen's arrest examples
1) PCSO Morris is out on foot patrol in his neighbourhood policing area. He is on his way to the local mosque as they have been subjected to hate crime in the past few weeks. As he approaches the building he sees a youth wearing a hooded top crouching down near the side wall of the mosque. The youth is spraying graffiti on the wall with a spray can. PCSO Morris shouts out and the youth looks in

his direction then runs off away from him. The officer gives chase and, as he runs past the wall, notices that the graffiti is offensive and racist. As he is running away, the youth trips and falls onto the pavement, providing PCSO Morris with the opportunity to catch up with and detain him. The officer tells the youth why he has detained him and calls for assistance using his personal radio. He is entitled to make a 'citizen's arrest' under Section 24A of PACE as an offence of racially or religiously aggravated criminal damage has been committed and the youth has been seen in the act of committing the offence. This particular offence is triable either-way (at the Magistrates' or Crown court) and, as such, is considered to be an indictable offence.

2) Mr Saunders is asleep in bed with his wife at home when he is woken by a noise from downstairs. The alarm clock shows the time as 3.40am. He gets up and creeps to the landing where he can see the light of a torch in the living room. He shouts to his wife to call the police and runs downstairs, where he is confronted by a man in dark clothing, holding the laptop computer which had been left in the study. The man tries to run towards the front door but Mr Saunders manages to grab hold of him and detains him on the floor. The man initially struggles but then gives up saying "okay mate, take it easy". When the police arrive Mr Saunders explains what has happened and hands the man over to the officers who arrest him and take him to the police station. When he is searched the police find a bank card belonging to Mrs Saunders in his trouser pocket. Mr Saunders discovers that the man had gained entry by forcing a UPVC window in the study. Mr Saunders is entitled to make a 'citizen's arrest' under Section 24A of

PACE as an offence of burglary has been committed and he has discovered the offender in the act of committing the offence. The offence of burglary is triable either-way (at the Magistrates' or Crown court) and, as such, is considered to be an indictable offence.

Other powers of arrest

Apart from the general power of arrest under Section 24 of PACE Act 1984, there are other powers of arrest;

- the common law power of arrest for breach of the peace has been preserved by Section 26 of PACE
- Section 27 of PACE provides a power of arrest to take a person's fingerprints
- Section 46A of PACE provides a power of arrest when a person fails to answer police bail
- Section 63A of PACE provides a power of arrest to take samples from a person in certain circumstances
- Sections 136–140 of the Criminal Justice and Public Order Act 1994 make provision for officers from one part of the UK to go into another part of the UK to arrest someone in connection with an offence committed within their jurisdiction. Under the 1994 Act an officer from a police service in England and Wales may arrest a person in Scotland where it appears that it would have been lawful for them to have exercised their powers had the suspected person been in their own policing area. Likewise, an officer from Scotland may arrest someone suspected of committing an offence in Scotland who is found in England, Wales or Northern Ireland if it would have been lawful to arrest that person had they been found in Scotland.

Arrest warrants

A warrant of arrest may be issued by Magistrates' or the Crown Court to secure the attendance of a person at that court and may also be issued to secure the attendance of a witness in certain circumstances.

Warrants issued in relation to an offence may be backed for bail, in which case the person is arrested then subsequently granted bail to appear at court. If the warrant is not backed for bail, the warrant will instruct that the person is brought before the next available court sitting. In these circumstances, the person will be held in custody at a police station until the specified court is able to receive them.

Warrants issued in connection with an offence do not need to be in the possession of the officer executing them at the time. It is enough simply to know that the warrant exists and to be provided with sufficient details to enable the officer to execute the warrant. The majority of warrants issued for the arrest of a person in England and Wales arise from matters such as failure to appear at court, breaching bail conditions or failing to pay fines. A number of these warrants are now enforced by civilian enforcement officers and approved enforcement agencies.

De-arrest

The term 'de-arrest' applies to situations where the police arrest a person in relation to an offence but then release them without taking them to the police station. This is perfectly lawful and covered by Section 30 PACE Act 1984 which states that 'A person arrested by a constable at any place other than a police station must be released without bail if, at any time before the person arrested reaches a police station, a constable is satisfied that there are no grounds for keeping him under arrest or releasing him on bail'.

De-arrest examples

1) A man is arrested for causing a breach of the peace at an address where there has been a disturbance. The officers establish that the man has another address some distance away where he can stay for the night. The man agrees to this course of action and is taken to the address by officers. As there is no longer a breach of the peace taking place and no likelihood of a recurrence, the man is de-arrested and given words of advice in relation to his future conduct.

2) Police are called to a fight outside a nightclub and upon arrival they see a group of three men who appear to be shouting aggressively and pushing each other. The situation is volatile and the officers decide to arrest all three for affray (a public order offence committed where 2 or more people use or threaten unlawful violence which would cause a person to fear for their personal safety). The men are put into separate police vehicles for transportation to the police station. On the way there, information is received following a review of the CCTV footage that one of the men was trying to split up a fight between the other two and hadn't actually committed an offence. He is de-arrested and volunteers to provide a witness statement to assist the investigation.

3) Police are called to an allegation of theft and are prevented from using a disposal other than arrest as the woman allegedly involved refuses to tell them her name or address, despite being warned of the potential consequences. As a

result of this, the officer considers it necessary to arrest the woman and informs her of the grounds and the reason why the arrest is necessary. She is put into the rear of a police car and as the vehicle leaves the scene she decides to disclose her name and address. The details are verified through police databases and she is de-arrested, released from detention and reported for the offence of theft.

Post-arrest

Section 30 of the PACE Act 1984 provides for the procedure to be adopted after a person has been arrested. The legislation states that an arrested person must be taken to a police station as soon as practicable after the arrest. The police station should be a 'designated' station (which has a custody suite and the capability to detain people securely) but there may be occasions when they are taken to a station which is not 'designated'. If this happens, the person should be released within six hours or taken to a 'designated' police station not more than six hours after their arrival at the first police station. The six hour timeframe is important as this is the period at which a person's detention is first reviewed following their arrest and authorised detention (see Detention – reviews). Section 30(10) allows for an officer to delay taking an arrested person to a police station where their presence elsewhere is 'necessary in order to carry out such investigations as it is reasonable to carry out immediately'. The delay will only apply if the matter requires an 'immediate' investigation, otherwise the person must be taken straight to a police station. The reasons for any delay must be recorded when the person first arrives at the police station. On arrival at the police station the detention process will begin.

The Authors' Reflections on the Topic

Stuart Gibbon

The taking away of a person's liberty is a huge step and one which must never be taken lightly. Although the Human Rights Act caters for such actions, any decision taken by the police or other law enforcement agency to arrest someone should be proportionate, lawful and necessary.

Prior to the introduction of the Police and Criminal Evidence Act 1984 (PACE) there were limited guidelines in relation to how an arrest should be effected and there is no doubt that the process of arrest, together with 'stop and search', was subject to abuse at times. The introduction of PACE, the associated Codes of Practice and other subsequent legislation has no doubt addressed a number of these issues. The police now have to specify why it has been necessary to arrest a person and are encouraged, where appropriate, to seek alternative methods such as voluntary interview or report for summons.

Police training schools across the UK rightly spend time in the classroom learning law and procedures as well as taking part in practical scenarios to hone their skills and decision-making. New recruits will be given the opportunity to practice their approach to making arrests in role-plays under the watchful gaze of experienced tutors. Valuable though this undoubtedly is, nothing can prepare you for the moment when you actually make your first arrest as a confirmed police constable. It's also a moment that you're unlikely to forget, no matter how many may follow during your police career. Mine was for being drunk and incapable, back in the 1980's, the prisoner that is, not me! Even though he wasn't interested in what I had to say and kept trying to kiss me, I had to make sure that I got the process right and remembered the caution. Feedback from my experienced colleagues and the opportunity to make further arrests, at that time mainly drunks and shoplifters, helped me to progress to the point where the process of making an arrest became almost second nature and just another part of 'the job'.

Stephen Wade

What impacts most clearly and dramatically on my responses to the notion of arrests and the legal arrest process in particular, is that, in the long years before we had professional police, how rare arrests were. J J Bagley comments on medieval law, for instance, which supports this response very solidly:

> 'One has only to leaf through the printed judicial records to get the impression that ordinary men and women in thirteenth century England lived in continual fear of danger and violence, and that their lives were often "nasty, brutish and short" Further study of the records merely strengthens one's first impressions. At Worcester in 1221, for example, the king's justices heard almost 200 cases of death or homicide, most of which were associated with robbery...'

In narratives from crime history, arrest is invariably of most interest when there is a context of riot and disorder. This is largely because of the consequences of an arrest in those difficult circumstances. Other versions of arrest which appeal to the writer and storyteller are those taking place in time of war or, as in Bamford's case, at a time of national paranoia.

As a writer, of course I want a story, and I want a story from the past which will still be powerful and intriguing today. For that reason, an arrest of a famous person is always appealing, and one such that really stands out is the occasion when Oscar Wilde was arrested at the Cadogan Hotel. The poet John Betjeman has played his part in making that arrest infamous. His poem 'The Arrest of Oscar Wilde at the Cadogan Hotel' raises several points about an arrest, and an outstanding one relates to the advent of the detective. The first professional detective force in Britain was created in 1842, and after that, plain clothes operations were hated by the public, being seen as 'foreign' and 'like spying.'

Betjeman uses this in the poem:
> *'A thump, and a murmur of voices –*
> *('Oh why must they make such a din?')*
> *As the door of the bedroom swung open*
> *And TWO PLAIN CLOTHES POLICEMEN came in:'*

Betjemen shows just how much drama and sensation may be involved in an arrest, rather than the usual 'soap' scene where the officer states the usual words, places an arm on the suspect, and then applies the cuffs. The other actors stare and there is an expectant silence, but none of that can compare with the impact of Betjeman's poem, which ends with a glimpse of poor Wilde: 'He brushed past the palms on the staircase/ and was helped to a hansom outside.'

My other mainstream reference conclusion is that as a historian, I inevitably compare our history with the history, ideologies and legal practices of other societies. I have found that, in order to understand the milieu around arrests in our history which are placed in the least humanitarian setting one might imagine, other stories from elsewhere open up understanding. In June 2020 for instance, Robert Irwin wrote an essay in *The Times Literary Supplement* describing his arrest in Israel in the 1970s. He wrote, '... two plain-clothes heavies turned up and escorted me from the room. I was escorted to a jeep in the back of which were two soldiers, both armed...'

That scenario could have been England in 1800, 1914 or 1940. The law exists to protect citizens, but an arrest is always going to be an ante-room to that place where the guilty reside. The arrested citizen already has suspicious looks: perhaps more revulsion than empathy.

Arrest and detention are two words that run through British history with a frisson of fear and apprehension; this has been so because they were either instruments of power from local or national supremos, or they were attached to repressive regimes with political elements.

Of course, there is also the subject of actions which, while they are not arrests, gather for enquiry as related concepts. In 2020 one of the most controversial of these is the actions of vigilantes. The word itself suggests the American Wild West and lawless gangs acting in terms of their own law – not the state's law. Within the last few years in Britain, for instance, vigilante groups have taken it upon themselves to entrap paedophiles by means of fabricating internet activity, posing as minors. One press account is careful with its choice of words: 'The court heard that vigilantes confronted......at the meeting and passed copies of the communication to the police...'

This 'confrontation' is surely in a grey area of the law. But the Supreme Court in July, 2020 ruled that the vigilante group did not breach the human rights of the alleged offender, with reference to the Article 8 of the European Convention on Human Rights. Through history, activities such as 'confronting' have always existed next door to actual arrests, and of course, the courts are kept busy as a result.

Bibliography

The literature of these topics is immense, and consequently the following is merely a selected list. In the historical materials, much of the relevant writing is in either the 'true crime' works or in those law texts that give case studies aimed at the general reader. We have omitted some of the rather formidable legal volumes intended for specialists.

Works Cited

Anon. *County Borough of Doncaster Special Constabulary* (Doncaster Borough Council, no date – probably 1940)

Baker, J.A., *An Introduction to English Legal History* (Butterworths, 2002)

Bamford, Samuel, *Passages in the Life of a Radical* (OUP, 1984)

Betjeman, John, *The Best of Betjeman* (John Murray, 1978)

Costin, W.C., and Watson, J. Steven, *The Law and Working of the Constitution*

Documents 1660–1914, Vol. 1 1660–1783 (Adam and Charles Black, 1961)

Denning, Lord, *Landmarks in the Law* (Butterworths, 1984)

Emsley, Clive, *The English Police: A Political and Social History* (Longman, 1996)

Halliday, Paul D., *Habeas Corpus: From England to Empire* (Belknap Press, 2010)

Hirst, Joseph H., *The Blockhouses of Kingston-Upon-Hull* (A. Brown, 1913)

Home Office Report of the Departmental Committee on Detective Work and Procedure (HMSO, 1938)

Moore, John, *Portrait of Elmbury* (Pan, 1952)

Richardson, John, *The Local Historian's Encyclopaedia* (Historical Publications, no date)

Saunders, John B., *Mozley and Whiteley's Law Dictionary* (Butterworth's, 1977)

Savill, Stanley, *The Police Service of England and Wales* (John Kempster, 1920)

Shakespeare, William, *Twelfth Night* in Lothian, J.M., and Craik, T.W., (editors) *Twelfth Night* (Routledge, 1988)

Sharpe, J.A., *Crime in Early Modern England 1550–1750* (Longman, 1999)

Thomas, Donald (Ed.) *State Trials: The Public Conscience* (Routledge and Kegan Paul, 1972)

Vickers, Kenneth H., *England in the Later Middle Ages* (Methuen, 1913

Other Citations

Latimer, Dr. J., 'Ancient Yorkshire Gallows' in William Smith (Ed.) *Old Yorkshire* (Longmans Green, 1889) pp. 51–54

Text of Magna Carta, 1215 produced by Rachel Sponar Harrison for the Directorate of Education and Cultural Services, Lincoln Castle (no date)

Additional Reference Works

Eddy, J.P., *Scarlet and Ermine* (William Kimber, 1960)

Earl of Birkenhead, *Famous Trials* (Hutchinson & Co., 1920)

Gray, John, *Lawyers' Latin* (Robert Hale, 2006)

Gregory, Jeremy, and Stevenson, John, *Britain in the Eighteenth Century* (Routledge, 2007)

Hibbert, Christopher, *The Roots of Evil* (Sutton, 2003)

Irving, Ronald, *The Law is an Ass* (Duckworth, 1999)

Macdonald, A.M., (Ed.) *Chambers Twentieth Century Dictionary* (Chambers, 1972)

Nield, Basil, *Farewell to the Assizes* (Garnstone Press, 1972)

Saul, Nigel, *A Companion to Medieval England 1066–1485* (Tempus, 2005)

Trilling, Lionel, and Bloom, Harold, *Victorian Prose and Poetry* (OUP, 1973

Articles and Essays
Ames, Jonathan, and Hamilton, Fiona, 'Paedophile Hunters did not breach Human Rights, Judges Rule' *The Times*, 17 July, 2020 p. 34
Irwin, Robert, 'One Night, in Jerusalem Jail' *Times Literary Supplement* June 19 2020 p.24

Online Sources
Generally, The Times Digital Archive and the other Gengage newspaper sources are always invaluable.
'Act for Abolishing Arrest for debt.' Times Digital Archive
'Arrest for Debt upon Mesne Process' *Hansard* 10 April 1827

Newspaper Sources
'Wrongful imposition of a curfew amounts to false imprisonment.' *Times Law Report* February 18 2020

Part 2

DETENTION

A prison wall was round us both,
*   Two outcast men we were:*
The world had thrust us from its heart,
*   And God from out His care;*
And the iron gin* that waits for sin
*   Had caught us in its snare*

Oscar Wilde: *The Ballad of Reading Gaol*

*Gin- gin-trap

Introduction

In a law report for February 18, 2020, the heading was, 'Wrongful imposition of a curfew amounts to false imprisonment.' The case was one about Ibrahima Jalloh, and the verdict was summed up in *The Times:*

> *'There was no need for the concept of imprisonment for the purposes of the common law tort of false imprisonment to be aligned with the concept of Deprivation of liberty under the right to liberty pursuant to article 5 of the European Convention on Human Rights.'*

A curfew had been imposed on Ibrahima Jalloh, and as he was released from jail, he was given a notice of restriction, and this pointed out that he was liable to be detained under the 1971 Immigration Act.

This case highlights the complexity of detention in all its forms in English law. First, in this case it was a tort (literally a 'wrong.'). In law it is defined as a civil wrong – so it is not within criminal law. Most commonly a tort will be featured in an action regarding a contract. But through history, the option of a civil action, when a criminal procedure has failed to satisfy the wronged claimant, has always been there. In modern times, one of the most celebrated instances has been in the prosecution of O J Simpson, who was acquitted of murder in a criminal trial but was later the subject of a civil action.

Through history, there have been detentions of all kinds, and each period and social context has its peculiar examples. Specific statutes have always been passed in order to allow the application of detention where there is a need, in the eyes of the forces of law and order. In 1952, for instance, the Prison Act established detention centres 'where persons of not less than fourteen but under twenty-one years of age may be detained for a disciplinary period suitable to their age and description.' This was to help solve the issue of 'contamination' whereby younger prisoners were lodged in jails with older prisoners.

But in order to show just how complicated the notion of detention becomes, it is interesting to look at two examples, one from Elizabethan times, featured in a Shakespeare play, and another from a police officer's memoir referring to an arrest in 1869. Both concern an issue of detention with mental health in view.

The first regards *Twelfth Night*. As research has shown, this was a play Shakespeare wrote for an audience of lawyers, and sure enough, he includes some humorous references to legal matters, but towards the close of the play, he includes an extraordinary sequence of events, all concerning the pretentious social climber, the steward of the Duchess, Malvolio. He has been duped and driven to distraction in an act of revenge engineered by Maria, the servant, and Sir Toby Belch, a wastrel who is the Duchess's uncle.

In Act III, scene iv, we have this:

Sir Toby: Come, we'll have him in a dark room and bound. My niece is already in the belief that he's mad; we may carry it thus for our pleasure, and his penance, till our very pastime, tired out of breath, prompt us to have mercy on him; at which time we will bring the device to the bar, and crown thee for a finder of madmen....

Malvolio has been detained. He has been imprisoned, probably in a cellar within the Duchess' mansion. He is a prisoner, utterly at the mercy of some captors, and he doesn't know the identity of these people. He is racked with fear, and helpless. In other words, he has been falsely imprisoned and treated in the same way as poor occupants of the London bedlam were treated in their insane states.

There has been no legal action or process. Malvolio has had no chance to exercise any rights. Nobody has helped him. There has not been a trial and a judgement. Of course, he has not broken the law; he has simply been arrogant and vain, imagining that his mistress the Duchess loves him, and he imagines being married to her.

Here the plot thickens, because should the servant marry the Duchess, then the social hierarchy is turned upside down – to the Elizabethan mind. He would own everything they had and he would govern her. The servant would become the master.

But this is a nasty, heartless and cruel trick to play on the man – being treated as if he were detained as a lunatic. Such acts of confinement run through history, and the second instances comes from an actual police memoir, written by John Pearman:

'Prisoner apprehended in London and brought to Windsor, the White Hart Hotel at 10.30 by two police officers from GSG 26 May charge withdrawn... warrant torn to pieces and destroyed by Capt. Farrer. Prisoner was kept at the Crown & Cushion, Eton in charge of police constables Critchlow and North...I took him to London by the GWR where he was examined by several doctors, then I took him to Paris, France where I arrived... and took him to an asylum where I left him...'

How extraordinary this narrative is. Sergeant Pearman escorted the prisoner to Paris in order for the man to be shut away for treatment. Before then he had been shuttled back and forth, while some kind of decision was made, and the warrant for his arrest (which was for fraud) was destroyed when it was accepted that the man was insane in some way. Now, this was done in a world in which mental illness was still little understood, and the borderline between criminality and insanity was blurred. There was a concept of 'criminally insane' and the destination for people with such labels was Broadmoor or similar.

The point here is that, like Malvolio, the arrested man (Reginald Murry) was dealt with without any mention of legal representation; he was treated like baggage, and the police were clearly very eager to have him out of the way and off their hands. He was detained in an asylum and that was the end of it.

Detention, then, has many aspects, and this first section of the book will cover aspects of prison, but also some instances where detention occurred in forms other than a time spent in what we today would understand as 'remand.'

Historical Perspectives: Stephen Wade

Case Studies: Prison and Asylum
In Solitary
Today, we know a lot about the effects of being 'in solitary.' The sociologist, Anthony Melechi, has summed up much of this knowledge, referring to studies on German prisoners in the late nineteenth century: '... medical investigators had

already confirmed that lack of sensory stimulation caused most prisoners in solitary confinement to become clinically insane within two years...' Placing someone in a box and regulating movement tends to erase sanity and invite rage, threats to identity and remove the stability humans need from their social and inter-personal essential behaviour.

Solitary confinement was central to the running of the gaols. The germ of this punishment lies in the gradual switch from a constant application of physical punishment to one of deprivation. By the 1820s the notion lay behind the latest concepts of rehabilitation, but in the local gaols which Howard saw, we have a good idea of how the refractory cells were used. The gaol registers at Maidstone show a typical range of cases. J Savage was confined to a dark cell for three days 'persuant to the order of the visiting magistrate' and 'Confined to a dark cell for three days, Mary Burrell, on the report from the matron that she had used improper language respecting the chaplain and for riotous conduct.' At the same gaol in 1821, William Constable and George Merchant were confined in dark cells, Constable for assaulting and beating James Styles, Merchant for singing in his sleeping cell.'

A survey of some instances of the application of solitary confinement in the years between c.1790 and 1830 shows that it was a controversial topic, but was generally accepted as the most severe punishment except for the lash. Some of the sentences given in court specified solitary rather than the usual gaol regime, as in the case of John Webb in 1828, who was in court for stealing three pewter pots from a pub in St James's. A female servant testified against him, and Webb, from the dock, took off a nailed shoe and violently threw it at her, striking her on the arm. The judge said that such an action deserved 'the heaviest penalty of the law' and that meant imprisonment in Newgate for six months, the whole time to be spent in solitary, and then that was to be followed by seven years of transportation.

Clearly, solitary confinement, though a regular short-term punishment in local gaols, was a special case in the general actions taken in sentencing. In 1816, William Price was sentenced at the West Sussex quarter sessions to six months solitary confinement on bread and water for stealing a leaden weight. It was also seen as an essential punishment for young criminals, with the attitude that it would deter them from further transgression. In 1831 at the Thames Police Court, an eleven-year-old girl called Isabella Brown was charged with stealing property from her employer in Commercial Road. The girl's mother begged the magistrates to do something to 'check the girl's propensity for pilfering' and the sentence was fourteen days in the house of correction to be in solitary confinement.

There were some voices of dissent and some were troubled by the idea of the 'dark cell.' In 1827 at the Surrey Asylum for the reformation of Discharged Prisoners there was a committee meeting at which this interchange took place:

'... an objection was placed by Mr Hedger to having persons placed in solitary confinement, conceiving the punishment too great. This mode of dealing with delinquents was stated to be very efficacious, and those who entered the Society had the rules read to them before they were admitted... The Honorary secretary said that at the Hoxton Institution, solitary confinement for offenders had done a great deal of good. It was at length agreed to, instead of using the words 'solitary confinement', 'separated from other inmates' should be substituted.'

This classic example of euphemism and double-think would have been ridiculous to the area of society in which solitary confinement was used most barbarically: in the army. In all the annals of corporal punishment in British imprisonment, arguably the most repulsive and savage use of solitary confinement was that described by an officer of the Royal Marines in a letter to the press in 1832. It concerns a private in the Royal North Lincolnshire Militia who, in 1804, struck at his sergeant-major with the butt-end of his musket. At a court-martial he was sentenced to 1,000 lashes and three months in solitary confinement in the black-hole of the main guardhouse. He was given the first 500 lashes and drummed out of the regiment.

Within the main prison estate, it was only at coroners' inquests that abuse and maltreatment of offenders came to public notice, and as is the same today, such an inquest involves an explanation of penal punishment. In 1825 at the notorious Millbank penitentiary, a young man called Lewis Abrahams hanged himself in his cell after what was alleged to have been ill treatment, including time in solitary. The Governor, Chapman, had to explain what his punishment regime was, and everything was examined, from the dietary to the small comforts allowed. The coroner asked what punishments were applied and Chapman said, 'There are three sorts.. the first and slightest is by taking away dinner and substituting bread and water; the next is confinement in a refractory cell into which the light is admitted by a very small window and the third and heaviest is confinement in a dark cell, and bread and water.... I can only continue these three days...'

Prison: Waiting in the Wings

Today, we think of the detention of the prisoner awaiting trial as a short period on 'remand' and in the prison, the remand prisoner will be housed on a separate wing, away from convicted inmates. This was not always the case.

The British have always been troubled by the questions of what prison is for and whether or not it works. That is, since the Victorian years. Before that, the dominant view of a prison is that it was where one sent the 'underclass' and those who transgressed. That seems very simple, but in fact it is much more complex, because those who broke the law were not all violent and dangerous types who would slit your throat as soon as look at you. Many unfortunates were debtors, victims of hard justice or incompetent lawyers, but at the heart of our prison history is a story of neglect and oblivion.

Until the Enlightenment thinkers and writers of the eighteenth century, there was very little thought given to the mass of people crammed into the gaols across the land. Throughout the medieval centuries, gaols were the province of local power bases, civil, military and ecclesiastical; later, after the creation of the first house of correction at Bridewell in London (hence the later generic term, 'Bridewell') in 1555, these gaols became business concerns, funded from local rates but existing to make a profit from convict labour.

The horror of the prison was primarily the thought of death from gaol fever: the early assize records list thousands of names of prisoners who died in gaol while waiting the assize trial; that means of course that a very large number of those deaths were of people awaiting trial. The history of our prisons is inextricably linked to

the growth of the assize court system and the story of
the assize courts is a reflection of how the criminal law
gradually developed and found a system which would have
parity across the land. The courts represent the boldest
step by which central legal power began to cover the King's
domains, using the local and the national elements together.
In each shire, the sheriff, who had been there since very
early times, gathered the jury and the other machinery of
law, ready for the visit of the assize judges, because that
is what assizes were – courts done in transit – giving the
assize towns distinguished visitors and a high level of ritual
and importance for a few days each year.

Originally, the law courts followed the King, and his own
court was the *Curia Regis.* Then in Magna Carta (1215) there
was this sentence: 'Common pleas shall not follow our Court
but shall be held in some certain place.' The result was that
Westminster was made that 'place' but then the notion of
having the top judges moving around to deal with criminal
and civil cases became a workable option, with economic
and logistical benefits of course, as persons accused would
be retained and then tried mostly in their own counties or
provinces.

The royal involvement and engagement with the system
may not always have been straightforward. Katherine
Harvey, writing about Henry III, has this comment:
'Henry was clearly (if understandably) unhappy about the
thirteenth century tendency to insist that the king must act
in accordance with the law, and was quick to defend his
rights.'

Since early Medieval times, there had been assizes –
literally 'sittings together' – to try causes and to gather
officials in the English regions to compile enquiries and

inventories into local possessions and actions. These were 'eyres' of assize, but they were not courts. The assize courts came when travelling justices went out into the counties to try cases: the Assize of Clarendon in 1166 and the Council of Northampton in 1196 decreed that the country should be split into six areas in which the judges of the High Court would sit. These became known as circuits.

In Edward I's reign an Act was passed to create court hearings in the local place of jury trial, before a summons for the jury to go to Westminster. The people involved were to come to London unless the trial had happened before: in Latin *nisi prius* (unless before). What developed over the centuries was that serious offences, crimes needing an *indictment*, had to be tried before a jury. The less serious offences, summary ones, could be tried by a magistrate. In addition to that, the terms *felony and misdemeanour* also existed until they were abolished in 1967: a felony was a crime in which guilt would mean a forfeiture of possessions and land, so the offender's children would lose their inheritance. A misdemeanour was a less serious crime. Prison sentences were therefore very different: felonies resulted in death, transportation or long sentences of hard labour.

The justices of assize had a number of powers. First, they had a commission of *oyer and terminer* (to listen and to act) on serious cases such as treason, murder, and any crime which was labelled a felony. They also had to try all people who had been charged and who had been languishing in gaol since their arrest, and they tried cases *nisi prius.* Basically, the judges would hear and sort out the cases relating to those languishing in gaol.

The assize circuits became established as the Home,

Midland, Norfolk, Oxford, Eastern, Western and Northern, and the records for these run from 1558 to either 1864 or 1876 when assizes were reorganised, or to 1971, when the assizes were abolished and crown courts created. From the beginning, the assize circuits covered all counties except Cheshire, Durham, Lancashire and Middlesex, the first three being referred to as the Palatinate Courts. In 1876, some courts moved from one circuit to another.

The result of all this means that a criminal who committed a crime in Leeds, for instance, after 1876, would be tried in Leeds rather than in York, the former seat of an assize for the West Riding. The assizes were held twice a year, from the thirteenth century until they ended in 1971, and these sessions were referred to as Spring and Winter. A third session could be held at times if the gaols were full – as in times of popular revolt and riots, or activities by gangs.

Court business was divided into two areas: for civil cases, referred to as 'crown' – and criminal cases. Two judges would be on the road, each with a responsibility for one of the two areas of law. In the law reports in *The Times*, these are clearly marked, in capitals. For instance, for the Winter Assizes in York in December, 1844, we have:

WINTER ASSIZES
NORTHERN CIRCUIT
YORK, DECEMBER 5.
(Before Mr Justice Coleridge)

The newspapers tend to use the terms, 'Crown side' and criminal side.' The judges arrived, and the hearings took place: the long line of prisoners, in irons, would stand before their learned lords, and some would be freed, some would be sent back to gaol, and some would be sentenced to hang.

The poor person waiting for trial could be sitting for months in a bug-infested, smelly and infected dark space, sometimes in irons and often on a starvation diet. The gaol fever was so extreme that it was common for judges, lawyers and anyone else in court to catch the fatal disease from the person in the dock. Deaths were regularly announced in the journals and periodicals; on several occasions, hundreds of men in the army died through gaol fever infection after one of their number rejoined the force after a spell in gaol.

The first real attempt to make the public aware of this terrible state of affairs was made by John Howard, a county sheriff and landowner who took upon himself the task of visiting the gaols across the land. The result was his book, *The State of the Prisons* (1777) which provides the kind of material we might expect in an official report, mixed with documentary insights. It is clear from Howard's writing that the local gaols and houses of correction were so determined on making a profit that they rarely considered the kinds of topics we discuss still today with regard to prison life: how first-time offenders and juveniles might be corrupted by old lags; how mental illness and deprivation mean that a prison is a place of care as well as of retribution, and how staff should have some kind of training for this special work.

Habeas Corpus and its Uses

The writ of habeas corpus is a legal instrument which commands that a captive and incarcerated subject of the sovereign be brought before a judge in order to ascertain the basis on which that person has been detained. As noted earlier, affairs of national security somewhat challenge and negate that writ. Vic Gatrell, in writing about the fears of the government in the 1790s with reference to social satire in the arts, explains this situation:

'In and after the 1790s, statutes multiplied to cover the common law's omissions. To start with, the king issued a proclamation against tumultuous meetings and seditious writings in 1792. A year later, habeas corpus was suspended after Louis XVI's guillotining, notwithstanding the fact that this prerogative writ is' unquestionably the first security of civil liberty.'

Matters were so ridiculous and outrageous that in 1795, because the king's coach was stoned, an Act was passed, and others followed, loosely termed the Convention Bills; these made gatherings of over fifty people 'treasonous.'

Writs, as will now have been appreciated, are at the core of measures taken to protect the sovereign's subjects. It is a serious topic, but law is swimming with stories and anecdotes, and one of these told is about a talented lawyer called Danckwerts which adds some lightness here; it concerns a trial at which there had been discussion as to which writ to issue, and Lord Alverstone said that 'all these remedies were much the same thing.' Then the tale has this:

'Above the din and bustle of the Court, Danckwerts was heard solemnly soliloquising, in the back row, in slow and measured tones:
..mandamus, a writ in the King's name commanding a specific act to be done. Quo warranto- a writ against a person or corporation that usurps a franchise. Prohibition,

a writ to forbid any court to proceed...and the Lord Chief Justice thinks that all these remedies are much the same thing. Oh Lord!'

Over the centuries, since the sixteenth century, the writ of habeas corpus has been applied in many ways. The writ always existed as a way to 'bring the body' of a person who had appealed to appear before the King's Bench, most often to be released, after a detention ordered by a lesser court. In other words, the King's subjects – the persons who were qualified to be helped by the writ – had royal protection from a variety of abuses, all of which might lead to being detained in custody.

Arguably, the most definitive study of habeas corpus in history is by Paul Halliday (see bibliography). Halliday gives a summary of the issue of these writs between 1500 and 1800, over which period he notes, 11,000 people used the writ. His summary explains that over those centuries, variations in numbers released from detention varied according to who was presiding over the Bench and also what larger matters from the 'big history' of particular times impinged on the writ's use.

Some of the work done by the writ was to counteract the effects of a line of repressive statutes; he locates one example which shows the kind of influence that might arise: 'After the Restoration...Those who violated the Five Mile Act, the Conventicle Acts or the Test Acts – which attempted to control preaching, worship and office holding by Protestant dissenters – often received a sympathetic hearing when habeas corpus brought them into King's Bench.'

Particularly in the Stuart and Georgian periods, it is strikingly significant that a writ to countermand something stemmed from a statute or from a pragmatic ruling from some abuse of power.

The following are some of the most prominent instances in which habeas corpus was applied or suspended. The latter is important because, of course, in times of emergency and crisis, the writ may be suspended, enabling the security forces to act quickly and without restraint. The really problematic issue in the history of habeas corpus is the fluctuations in effectiveness dependant on the pragmatism of emergency powers, the vulnerability of the land, and of course, the need for the internment of some elements of the population (as happened in the two world wars of the twentieth century).

Unlawful Detention in an Asylum

The Gentleman's Magazine in 1763 summed up what was going on. It noted that there were 'many unlawful arbitrary and cruel acts' happening in one of the proliferating private madhouses across the country. There had been some attempt to regulate these institutions, such as in the1774 Regulations of Madhouses Act, but there was still an attitude at that time towards 'lunatics' which was very much what Shakespeare depicted in *Twelfth Night.* People in families who were becoming a problem could be locked away, much as Bertha, Mr Rochester's wife, was in Jane Eyre, and Bertha was shut in a room with a nurse. Many other people were sent to the madhouses and left.

The legal issues around such detention were highlighted in the ongoing controversy, and the newspapers through the Georgian and Victorian times were often the channel for views such as this, from 1875, which told the story of Peter Chance:

'He was arrested as a pauper on the certificate of a medical man and two Justices. He was possessed at the time of an annuity of £143, besides other property and a business. He was arrested in the street on the 27th of March, 1874, and taken to the county asylum. The certificate was signed by Dr. Campbell, doctor of medicine at St Andrew's University, and was regular in form. There was no evidence that the relieving officer had been called in, and no reference whatever to the relieving officer.'

The relieving officer was the official in charge of supervising and issuing poor relief. As the Chairman of the Select Committee on the Lunacy Laws who heard the case of Mr. Chance, stated, 'Then the order was irregular on the face of it.' It certainly was. There was an enquiry, and it was found that Mr Chance was in the asylum for 31 weeks. He was discharged. But the horrific element in the case is that Mr Chance had to pay the immense sum of £600 for that release. (That sum would be in six figures today).

Actions for unlawful detention in asylums continued for decades, and there was always a cumbersome process involved to resolve the abuses.

Impressment
Through the centuries, Paul Halliday discusses in relation to habeas corpus, another detention was impressments into the Royal Navy. In the eighteenth century in particular, and into the Regency, Britain was often at war, and also had the expanding Empire to control. It was always in need of men. The press-gang was often in action, recruiting potential Jack tars either by the offer of 'The King's Shilling' or by force. The latter method was impressment. Paul Halliday recounts the case of two Dutchmen, Booy Booysen and John Brandt,

who were impressed in 1758 onto *HMS Princess Royal*. The men had been snatched from a merchant ship owned by one Frederick Franks, and his wife Mary.

Mary had writs composed and she tried to serve them to Captain Barber of the *Princess Royal.* Halliday writes that she 'tried to serve the writ... only to fail when the guards around his cabin stopped her. Undaunted, she returned the next day, when she was introduced to Lieutenant Crisp instead. She handed him the writ and explained what it was. Crisp paused, then dropped it and walked off...' This went on until the failure to serve was reported to Lord Mansfield, Chief Justice. The Captain and Crisp were in trouble. The Navy lawyers were told, and something had to be done.

Captain Barber was told that he must answer to all the consequences. That meant prison if reparations were not made; luckily for the Captain, the Navy eventually paid the bill, but he had a narrow escape from a long stay in a jail, where most inmates died of typhus.

The fact was that habeas corpus had to be returned. What happened at times when any kind of writ was issued was that an intermediary action was taken, by another writ being created. This was termed *mesne process*, and it happened in debt cases because there were so many vested interests in extorting whatever funds the wretched debtor might have- or that his family might have. A wealthy debtor was a good source of income for various parties.

State Security
As has been discussed in the first section of this book, with the story of Samuel Bamford, there have been plenty of occasions in the past in which national state security has overridden the rights of individuals. But equally, there are

many cases in which the fight has been lost, and illegal detention has won the day. This fact perhaps reveals one of the reasons why our fascination with the Tudor period goes on, as strong as ever. Also, in the early twentieth century, when MI5 emerged, the topic was again strongly immediate and sensational: what place individual freedom in a world threatened by destruction? How does the law fit in with the state emergency?

The very mention of the subject of detention and interrogation of captives in time of war is a source of embarrassment. This was made very clear with the publication of *The London Cage* by Lt. Col. A.P. Scotland in 1957. A note was placed after the table of contents: 'The War Office wishes to make it clear that the views and facts stated in this book are the author's own responsibility. Further, the War Office does not in any way vouch for the accuracy of the facts and does not necessarily accept any opinions expressed in this book.'

The suspension of habeas corpus opens up all kinds of angles on the workings of the law. When an Act is passed to such effect, the wording is of paramount interest, as we see in this extract, from the 1794 Habeas Corpus Suspension Act, which was an act to 'secure and detain such persons as his Majesty shall suspect are conspiring against his person and Government. It mentions a warrant and then that suspected persons '... may be detained in safe custody, without Bail or Mainprize,* until the first day of February, one thousand seven hundred and ninety-five; and that no judge or justice shall bail or try any such person... without order from his said Majesty's Privy Council.'

---

* Bail is freedom with sureties. Mainprize is an instruction to a sheriff to take sureties and release a person held.

In 1798 the act was repeated, but with an additional paragraph, and that shows the awareness from someone of a very extreme action in the earlier legislation. The new paragraph includes this: '... *the said persons so committed shall have the benefit and advantage of all laws and statutes any way relating to or providing for the liberty of the subjects of this realm...*'

Contemporary: Stuart Gibbon

During this section I'm going to talk about your time spent in police detention from arrival at the police station to your final disposal (sounds a bit dramatic but it just means what happens to you at the end of your detention). I'm going to explain the booking-in process, detention times and custody procedures, giving you practical examples for context. If you're a crime fan who wants to know what really happens in the confines of a custody suite or a writer who needs to get their facts right, this is a must read for you.

The powers to detain people who have been arrested and the manner in which they must be treated are contained in the Police and Criminal Evidence Act 1984 and the PACE Codes of Practice. The Codes are intended to protect the basic rights of detained people and, if they are followed by the police, it's more likely that evidence obtained whilst people are in custody will be admissible in court. The treatment of people who have been detained by police is mainly covered by PACE Code C. Any breach of this (or any) Code, although not necessarily unlawful, may adversely affect future legal process and render evidence unfair.

CASE LAW (R v Paul James Aspinall 1999)

A man was arrested near to a cache of drugs, his schizophrenia was confirmed by a medical examination, the doctor also indicating that he was fit to be interviewed. The man was interviewed without an appropriate adult or legal advice (the officer who allowed the interview to proceed was not aware of the man's mental illness): despite a psychiatrist confirming that it was possible that he was less able to cope with questions as a result of his illness and may have given answers which he thought were more likely to result in his release from custody (the interview took place after he had been in custody for some time). Despite these concerns the Judge allowed the interview to be admitted as evidence as, in their view, the man's apparent ability to deal with the interview obviated the need for an appropriate adult. The Court of Appeal overturned the subsequent conviction, finding that the Judge was wrong to admit the interview, inter alia because he had given too much weight to the man's apparent lucidity and not considered the purpose of the safeguard of an appropriate adult, including the latter's role in considering the question of legal advice being obtained. Since it was clear that the man should have had an appropriate adult, it was unfair to have admitted the interview evidence, particularly as the interview had taken place without legal advice. The failure to follow the requirements to have an appropriate adult present at the interview of a person with mental health issues (breaching Code C) meant that, despite the man's apparent lucidity, the interview contents were considered to have been unfairly obtained and were inadmissible as evidence.

Transport

If you've been arrested by the police the chances are that you will be taken to a police station in a marked police car or van. If you're arrested by a detective or an officer working in plain clothes then your mode of transport will probably be an unmarked police car. If you're in a CID car then it is likely to be a fairly standard vehicle such as a Ford Focus or a Peugeot and is likely to be a neutral colour such as black, dark blue or red rather than white or yellow. An unmarked traffic car will probably be a BMW or an Audi.

Arrival at the police station

In recent years there have been well-publicised cuts to police officer numbers and closures of police stations which have had an adverse impact on policing in general. The amount of custody officers and the availability of designated police stations, with fully operational custody suites, have both reduced. This has resulted in police officers often having to travel some distance with the arrested person and having to wait in a queue upon arrival so that they can be processed. It's not uncommon for arresting officers to have to wait in the police station yard with the arrested person in the back of their vehicle until their turn to enter the custody suite. Police stations also usually have a secure holding area designed for arrested persons prior to booking in.

Custody officer

The main responsibility for a detained person lies with the custody officer but all staff must be aware of the provisions of the PACE Act and the Codes of Practice. The custody officer is responsible for the reception and treatment of prisoners detained at the police station. Their role is to act independently of the investigating officers and to look after the welfare and rights of the detained person. A custody officer must be an officer of at least the rank of Sergeant and, although officers of higher ranks are permitted to carry out the role, in reality it's usually a uniformed Sergeant. In fact, if an officer of a higher rank were to perform the role when there was a trained Sergeant (with no other role to perform) available at that police station, this may be considered unlawful. At one time the custody officer would be responsible for completing the whole of the booking-in process and many other tasks, assisted by a uniformed constable, but these days they are supported by other staff.

Custody support staff

Some of the roles which used to be carried out by the custody officer and other uniformed colleagues are now performed by custody support staff. They are not police officers but have been given the authority to carry out certain tasks within the custody area. They wear a standard uniform and will have their title printed on their shirt epaulettes or on the sleeve of their shirt. Their formal role title is Designated Detention Officer (DDO) or Custody Detention Officer (CDO). They carry out a number of tasks which include providing assistance with the booking-in process, checking on the welfare of detainees, making phone calls to solicitors and outside agencies and, in some forces, taking samples such as fingerprints and DNA swabs. In a busy custody suite you are likely to find a number of support staff and more than one custody officer.

Custody record

Whenever a person is brought to a police station under arrest, is arrested at the police station having attended there voluntarily or attends a police station to answer bail they must be brought before the custody officer as soon as practicable after their arrival or following their arrest. A separate custody record must be opened for each person arrested which should be continually updated during their time in police detention. Although the records are computerised they are capable of being printed out in a paper format when required. The detainee's solicitor and appropriate adult (if required) must be allowed to inspect the custody record during the period of detention. When a detainee leaves police detention or is taken before a court they, their legal representative or appropriate adult shall be given, on request, a copy of the custody record as soon as practicable. This entitlement lasts for 12 months after release. A custody record should be accurate and comprehensive as it may well be scrutinised months or even years after the detainee has been released from custody.

Rights

The arresting officer will be asked to provide the details of and grounds for the arrest in the presence of the arrested person and the custody officer. If the arrested person is too violent or otherwise unfit then this may not be possible at the time but should be re-visited when appropriate. Having heard the information, the custody officer must decide whether or not there are reasons which justify authorising that person's detention. If there is insufficient evidence available at that time to charge the person then the custody officer may authorise their detention in order to secure and preserve evidence or obtain evidence by questioning. Detention may be authorised for one or both of those reasons. The detained person will then be given their rights as follows;

i)   the right to consult privately with a solicitor and that free independent legal advice is available
ii) the right to have someone informed of their arrest
iii) the right to consult the Codes of Practice
iv) if applicable, the right to interpretation and translation and the right to communicate with their High Commission, Embassy or Consulate

The detained person must also be given a written notice containing information about their rights and detention. The custody officer will say something along the lines of "I've heard the reasons and grounds for your arrest and I'm authorising your detention at this police station to secure and preserve evidence and to obtain evidence by questioning in the form of an interview. Whilst you're here you have certain rights. You have the right to have someone told that you have been arrested, you have the right to consult with a solicitor, free of charge, and you have the right to consult with the Codes of Practice, which is a book about police practices and procedures, during your detention. You can do any of those things now but if you choose not to you can still do them at any time whilst you're here". The custody officer will then ask the detained person whether they wish to exercise any of those rights at that time and will note their response and request a confirmatory signature.

You will see that one of the rights is to 'have someone informed of their arrest' and, despite some contrary views, this is not the same as 'being entitled to a phone call'. Depending on the circumstances, you may be allowed to make a call whilst in custody which will be strictly monitored by custody staff via speakerphone but, in the majority of cases, the custody staff will make the phone call on your behalf. They will tell the recipient that you have been arrested and which police station you're at, but not why you have been arrested nor any information about the circumstances.

Searching

The custody officer is responsible for establishing what property a detained person has with them when they come to the police station and the safekeeping of any property taken from that person which remains at the police station. For this reason, the custody officer may search that person or authorise their being searched to the extent they consider necessary. A detained person may retain clothing and personal effects at their own risk unless the custody officer considers they may use them;

• to cause harm to themselves or others
• interfere with evidence
• damage property
• effect an escape, or
• they are needed as evidence

The custody officer may withhold such articles as they consider necessary and must tell the detained person the reason(s) why. Personal effects are those items a detained person may lawfully need, use or refer to while in detention but do not include cash and other items of value.

The custody officer may only authorise a search to the extent that they consider necessary. In order to safeguard the rights of the detained person, there are three levels to which searches can be conducted;

- searches that do not involve the removal of more than the detained person's outer clothing (this includes shoes and socks)
- strip searches
- intimate searches

The most common search which applies to almost every person who comes before the custody officer doesn't require the removal of more than outer clothing. This type of search would normally involve emptying pockets, removing jewellery and searching outer clothing such as jackets and a 'pat down' of the detained person. Not all detained persons need to be searched so if it is clear that they will only be detained for a short time and not placed in a cell, the custody officer may decide not to search them and will simply record this fact on their custody record.

Strip search

A strip search is a search involving the removal of more than outer clothing and covers everything from the removal of a shirt or trousers to the removal of all clothing. This type of search may take place only if it is considered necessary to remove an article which a detained person would not be allowed to keep and the officer reasonably considers the detained person might have concealed such an article. They should not be routinely carried out unless there is proper justification. A police officer carrying out a strip search must be the same sex as the detained person. The search should take place in an area where the detained person cannot be seen by anyone who doesn't need to be present, nor by a member of the opposite sex (except an appropriate adult specifically requested by the detained person). In all but the most urgent cases, whenever a strip search involves exposure of intimate body parts, there must be at least two people present other than the detained person. A strip search should be conducted as quickly as possible and the detained person should be allowed to dress as soon as the search has been completed. Every reasonable effort should be made to minimise embarrassment and detainees should not normally be required to remove all their clothes at the same time, instead removing clothing above the waist then re-dressing before removing further clothing. A strip search requires the authority of the custody officer.

Strip search examples
Shaw is found in possession of a bag of white powder which is believed to be cocaine. He is arrested on suspicion of the possession of a controlled drug and taken to the police station. On the way to the station, although handcuffed, he appears to be fidgeting constantly. A check of the Police National Computer (PNC) reveals that he has previously secreted drugs in his clothing. Due to this information and Shaw's behaviour the custody officer authorises a strip search. Further small wraps of powder are found in his socks and underwear.

Wilson is arrested for threatening to kill a paramedic. It becomes clear that she has mental health issues and is a suicide risk. The custody officer orders the removal of her clothing so that she can be dressed in a safety gown. During this process the items of clothing are searched and a razor blade is found taped to the inside of her bra.

Intimate search

An intimate search consists of the physical examination of a person's body orifices other than the mouth. The intrusive nature of such searches means that the actual and potential risks associated with intimate searches must never be underestimated.

Body orifices other than the mouth may be searched only:

(a) if authorised by an officer of inspector rank or above who has reasonable grounds for believing that the person may have concealed on themselves:

(i)   anything which they could and might use to cause physical injury to themselves or others at the station; or

(ii) a Class A drug which they intended to supply to another or to export;

(iii) and the officer has reasonable grounds for believing that an intimate search is the only means of removing those items; and

(b) if the search is under paragraph (a)(ii) (a drug offence search), the detainee's appropriate consent has been given in writing.

Before a detainee is asked to give consent to a drug offence search they must be warned that if they refuse without good cause, such a refusal may harm their case if it comes to trial. This warning, which may be given by a police officer or member of police staff, should be given in the following form of words – **You do not have to allow yourself to be searched, but I must warn you that if you refuse without good cause, your refusal may harm your case if it comes to trial**.

An intimate search may only be carried out by a registered

medical practitioner or registered nurse, unless an officer of at least Inspector rank considers this is not practicable and the search is to take place under paragraph (a)(i) (physical injury search), in which case a police officer may carry out the search. A constable should only be authorised to carry out an intimate search as a last resort and when all other approaches have failed. A full written record should be made on the custody record of all considerations, rationale and the actions taken.

CASE STUDY – INTIMATE SEARCH
A custody Sergeant "overstepped the mark" by performing an "intimate search" on a suspected Class A drug dealer, a police watchdog has reported. West Mercia Police referred the case to the Independent Office for Police Conduct (IOPC), and have agreed to provide refresher training for officers handling detainees. An IOPC report says the Sergeant was permitted to 'strip search' the suspect due to their demeanour and history but proceeded to carry out a more thorough search "without appropriate authorisation". Investigators examined the custody record and interviewed the custody sergeant and detainee. Their report concluded "In our opinion, the custody Sergeant had intended to conduct a strip search and had unwittingly extended beyond the parameters and performed an intimate search without appropriate authorisation. We did not believe there was evidence the custody Sergeant had deliberately sought to conduct an intimate search without authorisation. We were also of the opinion that there wasn't enough reason to conduct an intimate search – even though the custody Sergeant stated that he had performed the search with the welfare of the detainee in mind. Based on the evidence

available, we were of the opinion that the custody Sergeant may have a case to answer for misconduct. Our investigation highlighted a need for the force to implement additional or refresher training for officers who move into a custody environment, to be delivered before they commence their roles. After reviewing our report, West Mercia Police agreed that the Sergeant had breached the standards of professional behaviour. The force considered that the Sergeant had acted in good faith and had demonstrated a degree of insight, reflecting on his actions, and conceding he had overstepped the mark. They proposed to deal with this through management action".

Risk assessment

When a police officer makes an arrest, they are personally responsible for the assessment of risk and welfare of the detained person. This responsibility continues until the detained person is handed over to the custody officer at the police station. A risk assessment includes the risk and potential risk that a detained person presents to themselves, police staff, other detainees and others with reason to enter the custody suite area. A risk assessment is likely to be continuous and needs to respond to changing situational requirements. It may be impractical for such an assessment to be written, particularly in dynamic situations, but actions taken and rationale should be documented at the earliest opportunity.

The custody officer is responsible for the documentation and recording of a risk assessment for every detainee who is presented before them. This process will take place in the very early stages of their detention (unless impractical by reason of the behaviour or condition of the detainee) and will usually follow the recording of personal details such as name, address and date of birth. The custody or detention officer must ensure that the detainee is asked a number of questions including the following:

- Do you have any illness or injury (including asthma, diabetes, heart condition)?
- Have you seen a doctor or been to a hospital for this illness or injury? (if affirmative)
- Are you experiencing any mental ill health or depression?
- Would you like to speak to the doctor/nurse/paramedic? (as appropriate)
- Are you taking or supposed to be taking any tablets or medication? If yes, what are they and what are they for?
- Have you ever tried to harm yourself? If yes, how often, how long ago, how did you harm yourself, have you sought help?
- Have you consumed alcohol or non-prescribed drugs recently?
- Do you have any drug/alcohol dependency?
- Do you require help with reading, writing or have learning disabilities?
- Do you have any special dietary or religious needs?

If the detainee answers 'yes' to any of the above, they should be asked further questions and be provided with the appropriate support.

These questions should be asked in a manner which encourages and elicits information. The answers given will identify any medical or other requirements and will assist the custody officer in making informed decisions about continued detention. For example, a detained person who is identified as a suicide risk will, if placed in a cell or other detention room, be subject to 'constant watch' and will be monitored by a police officer/staff sitting directly outside the open door at all times.

Delay in notifying arrest or allowing access to legal advice (Sections 56 & 58 PACE Act)

In certain limited circumstances, the exercise of the right to have someone informed of your arrest and/or the right to have access to legal advice may be delayed if you are in police detention in connection with an indictable offence (triable at Crown court), have not yet been charged with an offence and a senior officer has reasonable grounds for believing their exercise will:

(i) lead to:
- interference with, or harm to, evidence connected with an indictable offence; or
- interference with, or physical harm to, other people; or

(ii) lead to alerting other people suspected of having committed an indictable offence but not yet arrested for it; or

(iii) hinder the recovery of property obtained in consequence of the commission of such an offence

These rights may also be delayed if the officer has reasonable grounds to believe that:

(i) the person detained for an indictable offence has benefited from their criminal conduct; and

(ii) the recovery of the value of the property constituting that benefit will be hindered by the exercise of either right.

The authority of an Inspector or above is required to delay the notification of an arrest and the authority of a

Superintendent or above is required to delay access to legal advice. Both delays interfere with the fundamental rights of a detained person and should only be exercised when absolutely necessary. The rights may be delayed only for as long as grounds exist and in no case beyond 36 hours. Authority to delay a detainee's right to consult privately with a solicitor may be given only if the authorising officer has reasonable grounds to believe that the solicitor which the detainee wants to consult with will, inadvertently or otherwise, pass on a message from the detainee or act in some other way which will have any of the consequences specified. The fact that the grounds for delaying notification of arrest may be satisfied does not automatically mean that the grounds for delaying access to legal advice will also be satisfied. If the detainee wishes to see a solicitor, access to that solicitor may not be delayed purely on the grounds they might advise the detainee not to answer questions or that the solicitor was initially asked to attend the police station by someone else. It's rare for these fundamental rights to be denied or delayed but it sometimes happens. In such cases the custody record must be updated with reasoning and comments from the authorising officer.

CASE LAW (R v Samuel 1988)

A man was arrested on suspicion of robbery and when given his rights he requested a solicitor. The police refused, claiming such access might lead to the suppression of evidence or the warning of accomplices. At a subsequent police interview, in the absence of a solicitor, the suspect made admissions which were later given in evidence. The Court of Appeal found in favour of the arrested person, reinforcing that Section 58(8) allowed the right to legal advice to be delayed only where the police have reason to believe that allowing access to a particular solicitor (not just any solicitor) will (not might) have the undesirable consequences listed. Since this was not the case, and since the defendant's solicitor testified that he would have advised the defendant not to make any admission, the conviction was quashed.

R v Vernon (1988)

A woman was arrested for assaulting a neighbour late one night and arrived at the police station after midnight. She asked to see a particular solicitor but, on being told that this solicitor was not available, she agreed to be interviewed without legal advice rather than wait until later that morning. The police did not tell the woman that there was a duty solicitor already on his way to the police station to see another detainee. At her trial, the Judge said it was clear that she would have waited had she known the duty solicitor would be present soon, and the police had a duty to tell her this. In the circumstances, her interview was excluded.

R v Alladice (1988)

A man was arrested for armed robbery at a post office and, when given his rights, requested a solicitor. He was well aware of his legal rights and wanted a solicitor only as an independent witness. The police refused to contact a solicitor and the man was subsequently convicted on the evidence, which included his own admissions. Dismissing his appeal, the Court of Appeal determined that there had been a breach of Section 58 PACE Act in that the proper grounds for refusal had not been established, but found that the presence of a solicitor would have added nothing to the defendant's knowledge of his rights and there was no reason for his admissions to have been excluded.

Appropriate adult

The PACE Act introduced the role of the appropriate adult as a safeguard to reduce the risk of miscarriages of justice as a result of evidence obtained from vulnerable suspects which, by virtue of their vulnerability, led to unsafe and unjust convictions. Any person under the age of 18 or anyone else of any age, whom an officer has reason to suspect may be vulnerable, must have an appropriate adult present at the police station to advise, support and assist them. In the case of a person who is vulnerable, 'the appropriate adult' means:

(i)   a relative, guardian or other person responsible for their care or custody;

(ii) someone experienced in dealing with vulnerable persons but who is not;
  - a police officer;
  - employed by the police;
  - under the direction or control of the chief officer of a police force;
  - a person who provides services under contractual arrangements (but without being employed by the chief officer of a police force), to assist that force in relation to the discharge of its chief officer's functions, whether or not they are on duty at the time.

(iii) failing (i) or (ii), some other responsible adult aged 18 or over who can take an interest in their welfare.

An appropriate adult should be present when a child or other vulnerable person is given their rights and, if they are not, those rights should be repeated in their presence when they arrive at the police station. Their role does not include the provision of legal advice but they can request such advice if they feel that it is required. The appropriate adult will be present during any police interview and is not expected to act simply as an observer. Their purpose during the interview is to advise the interviewee, observe whether or not the interview is being conducted properly and fairly and to facilitate communication with the interviewee. They are not there to answer questions on behalf of the interviewee but to make sure that the question is fully understood and that any answer is communicated effectively. In most cases, the appropriate adult will be a parent, guardian, a trained worker from children or adult services, or a member of an approved appropriate adult scheme run by the local authority.

CASE LAW (R v Blake 1989)

A 16 year old girl suspected of arson asked for her social worker to be present rather than her estranged father. The social worker refused to attend as a matter of policy and the girl was interviewed in the presence of her father after all. The High Court criticised the Social Services' policy decision and ruled that the subsequent confession must be excluded on the basis that the appropriate adult must be someone in whom the vulnerable person has confidence.

R v Morse (1991)

A 16 year old boy was arrested for arson and his father attended the police station as appropriate adult. They declined legal advice and the boy went on to make various admissions during a police interview. At trial, the Judge accepted an application by the defence that the admissions should be excluded as evidence. Both the boy and his father were of low intelligence and it appeared that the father had not understood the seriousness of his son's position. The police had behaved impeccably, but the test for an appropriate adult was an objective one, and the prosecution could not show that the boy's confession was reliable.

Continuing detention

When a person is in police detention there is a requirement that their continuing detention is regularly reviewed. A lot of people arrested by the police are detained for less than six hours and most other cases are concluded within 24 hours. In some cases, detention is required for more than 24 hours. I'm going to explain how long the police can detain you, how and when your detention will be reviewed and when the police may need to attend court to apply for further time.

Relevant time

The PACE Act and the Codes of Practice make reference to the 'relevant time' which is the time from which the limits of detention are calculated. The 'relevant time' of a person's detention starts in accordance with Section 41(2)–(5) of the PACE Act which states:

(2) The time from which the period of detention of a person is to be calculated (the 'relevant time') –

    (a) in the case of a person to whom this paragraph applies shall be –

        (i) the time at which that person arrives at the relevant police station; or

        (ii) the time 24 hours after the time of that person's arrest, whichever is the earlier;

(b) in the case of a person arrested outside England and Wales, shall be –

(i) the time at which that person arrives at the first police station to which he is taken in the police area in England or Wales in which the offence for which he was arrested is being investigated; or

(ii) the time 24 hours after the time of that person's entry into England and Wales, whichever is the earlier.

There are other subsections which relate to voluntary attendance and being transferred between different police force areas but the above are probably the most common. In a nutshell, if you are arrested in England or Wales then the 'relevant time' is likely to be when you arrive at the police station where you are going to be dealt with unless it takes more than 24 hours to get there, in which case the 'relevant time' will be 24 hours after your arrest. If you are arrested outside England and Wales then it will be the time that you arrive at the police station investigating your offence in England or Wales or 24 hours after your entry into England and Wales, whichever comes first.

Relevant time examples

1) A person is arrested in Manchester and taken to their local designated police station where the offence is to be investigated. The 'relevant time' will be the time this person arrives at that police station.

2) A person is arrested in Cumbria as they are circulated as wanted by the police in Cornwall. They are lodged at a police station in Cumbria overnight and not questioned about the offence in question. The next day they are taken

to Cornwall, arriving more than 24 hours after their arrest. The 'relevant time' will be the time 24 hours after arrest.

3) A person is arrested in Glasgow as they are wanted in Oxford. They are taken to Oxford in a police vehicle. The 'relevant time' will be the time of arrival at the police station in Oxford where the offence is being investigated or the time 24 hours after entry into England, whichever is the earlier time.

Review of police detention

During a person's detention there is a requirement for the circumstances to be regularly reviewed to establish whether continued detention is lawful and justified. If a person has been arrested but not charged, that review will be carried out by an officer of at least the rank of Inspector, not connected with the investigation of the offence (most of the time it will be an Inspector but it could be an officer of a higher rank if there were no Inspectors available). There are written guidelines which outline when these reviews should be carried out. The first review should be not later than six hours after the detention of the person was first authorised. The second review should be not later than nine hours after the first. Subsequent reviews should be at intervals of not more than nine hours. The total number of reviews carried out on a person in detention will depend on how long they spend in custody. If a person has been arrested, charged with an offence and remains in custody to be brought before the next available court, their post-charge reviews will be carried out by the custody officer (Sergeant).

Review example

Newton is arrested at 10.00am and his detention is authorised at 10.30am. His first review should be no later than 4.30pm. If he was still in custody beyond that time, his next review should be no later than 1.30am the following morning. If a detainee is likely to be in a period of rest (an 8 hour period free from interruption) when a review is due, the review can be brought forward to allow the full rest period. So, in this example, the second review may be carried out at 11.00pm (rather than 1.30am). This would mean that the next review would be due no later than 8.00am the next morning (no more than nine hours later).

Extended detention without charge

A significant amount of detained people are dealt with in less than 24 hours but it may be necessary for them to be detained for longer. This may apply if the case is serious and/or complex. Section 42 PACE Act 1984 states that detention can only be authorised beyond 24 hours and up to a maximum of 36 hours from the 'relevant time' if :

- an offence being investigated is an 'indictable offence'; and
- an officer of the rank of Superintendent or above is responsible for the station at which the person is detained; and
- that senior officer is satisfied that:
  - there is not sufficient evidence to charge; and
  - the investigation is being conducted diligently and expeditiously; and
  - the person's detention is necessary to secure or preserve evidence relating to the offence or to obtain such evidence by questioning that person.

Although the authorising officer can authorise detention up to a maximum of 36 hours, the period may be shorter than this. If they are not satisfied that the investigation is being progressed satisfactorily they can refuse the application. Alternatively, they may authorise part, but not all, of the additional 12 hours, for example they may authorise an extra 6 hours or 9 hours. If the authorising officer doesn't grant the full 12 hour extension, a further application can be made subsequently, if justified, but cannot exceed the 36 hour detention period. From an investigating officer's perspective, the timing of the application is very important as the 'detention clock' is continuously running. The authority must be granted after the 15th hour of detention but before the expiry of 24 hours, in other words after the second review but before the third review.

To summarise, the decision to detain a person up to 24 hours without charge is made by an Inspector. If the investigating officer wishes to keep the person in detention for longer than 24 hours they must seek the authority of a Superintendent who can, if satisfied, authorise up to a further 12 hours detention, which would take the total detention time to 36 hours.

Warrant of further detention

Section 43 of the PACE Act explains the procedure when police seek to keep a person in detention for longer than 36 hours. An application must be made to a Magistrates court who can, if satisfied that further detention is justified in the circumstances, issue a warrant of further detention for a specified additional period. This period can be up to, but no longer than, 36 hours (which would take the total detention time to 72 hours). The criteria for an application is exactly the same as for the Superintendent's extension and the Magistrates may grant the full amount requested by the police or part of it. The application must be made before the expiry of the first 36 hours in custody but, if it isn't practicable for the Magistrates court to sit within the 36-hour period, the application can be made within the following 6 hours. The detainee and their solicitor, if legally represented, should be present at court and the latter will have the opportunity to challenge the application and question the police officer making the application.

Extended warrant of further detention

Section 44 of the PACE Act provides for a Magistrates court to extend a warrant of further detention up to a maximum of 96 hours from the time at which the detainee first arrived at the police station. The criteria and process is exactly the same as for the warrant of further detention and the application must be made to the court before the expiry of the extension granted in the previous warrant. Once the authorised period of additional detention has expired the detainee must be charged or released.

Detention in Scotland

The Criminal Justice (Scotland) Act 2016 deals with arrest and detention in Scotland. If you are arrested without warrant under Section 1 of the Act, but have not been charged or reported to the Crown Office and Procurator Fiscal Service, you will be referred to as 'Not Officially Accused'. If your detention has been authorised by the custody Sergeant you may only be detained initially for a maximum of 12 hours, beginning with the time at which authorisation was given (Section 9). At the conclusion of those 12 hours you must be charged or released unless the police can justify a continued period of detention. A further 12 hour period can be authorised by a police Inspector (if you are 18 or over) or Chief Inspector (under 18) provided certain conditions are met (Section 11);

- there are reasonable grounds for suspecting you have committed an offence
- keeping you in custody is necessary and proportionate to bring you to court or deal with you in accordance with the law
- the offence in question is an indictable offence and the investigation is being conducted diligently and expeditiously

In summary, the maximum period of detention without charge in Scotland is 24 hours.

The term 'Officially Accused' relates to a person who has been arrested without warrant under Section 1 of the Criminal Justice (Scotland) Act 2016 and has been charged or reported to the Crown Office and Procurator Fiscal Service. When a person who is 'Officially Accused' is arrested and taken into police custody, they may be held in detention until they can be brought before a court.

Identification checks and samples

When you are booked into custody you will be asked to give your personal details including your name, address and date of birth. This information will be searched on a number of databases including the Police National Computer (PNC) to assist with the risk assessment. The police also have the power to take some samples from you without your consent. This process will usually take place shortly after you have been booked in and will be carried out by a member of police detention staff or, in some cases, a police officer.

Your fingerprints will be taken using a digital machine, probably Live Scan, which captures an image of your prints, scans them, and electronically searches them against a national database. This method is inkless and extremely fast, confirming identification in a matter of minutes. Anyone who provides false personal details to the custody staff, because they are wanted for other offences perhaps, won't be able to evade justice for long.

Your photograph will be taken and stored on a retrievable database. A head-on and side view image will be captured and you will be asked to remove any headgear or other item which may alter your appearance. Every time you are arrested your photograph will be taken.

A sample of your DNA will be taken using a buccal swab (a bit like a cotton bud) which is rubbed against the inside of your cheeks then packaged and securely stored. This sample will be sent off and the resulting DNA profile will be entered onto the National DNA Database. The profile will also be searched against any unidentified crime scene stains relating to unsolved crimes where DNA (such as from blood or saliva) was recovered but has yet to be attributed to an individual.

Footwear impressions will also be taken using an inkless method which is likely to require you to stand on or walk over a pad or low platform so that the tread of your footwear can be captured. The impressions will be searched against a database of outstanding footwear marks left at crime scenes. Footwear evidence will often provide supporting evidence rather than the sole (pardon the pun!) evidence in a case but can be particularly important in cases of burglary and robbery. The advanced techniques available to Crime Scene Investigators (CSI's) these days increase the likelihood of the retrieval of good quality footwear marks.

CASE STUDY – FOOTWEAR MARKS
A burglar has been jailed thanks to footwear evidence linking him to the crime. Daniel Prague has been sent to prison for breaking into a house in Weeton in May 2019. In the early hours of the morning, the occupants discovered that a window had been forced open and property had been stolen. Shortly after, Prague and another man were arrested nearby on suspicion of burglary after being shown acting suspiciously on CCTV. They refused to answer questions during a police interview and their clothing and footwear were seized before they were released under investigation. A forensic scientist was able to analyse the pattern, the general wear and damage features of Prague's footwear and match it to that of a footprint found at the burgled property. Prague again provided a 'no comment' interview and was charged with burglary. In November 2019 at York Crown Court, Prague pleaded guilty to burglary and was sentenced to 13 months in prison. The investigating officer from North Yorkshire Police CID commented "This case demonstrates how advancements in forensic analysis are helping us to link offenders to their crime and prove their guilt, even when they continue to maintain their innocence."

Forensic samples
During your time in police detention you may be asked to provide sample(s) to assist the investigation. This will depend on the type of offence you have been arrested for and will usually only apply to sexual offences, assaults and property offences such as burglary and robbery. There are

two types of samples which have different authority levels and criteria.

Intimate sample

An intimate sample means a dental impression or sample of blood, semen or any other tissue fluid, urine, or pubic hair, or a swab taken from any part of a person's genitals or from a person's body orifice other than the mouth.

Section 62(1) of the PACE Act provides that intimate samples may be taken from a person in police detention only:

(i)   if a police officer of Inspector rank or above has reasonable grounds to believe such an impression or sample will tend to confirm or disprove the suspect's involvement in a recordable offence, and gives authorisation for a sample to be taken; AND

(ii) with the suspect's written consent

There are other sub-sections of Section 62 which relate to the taking of intimate samples when a person is not in police detention.

Dental impressions may only be taken by a registered dentist. Other intimate samples, except for samples of urine, may only be taken by a registered medical practitioner, nurse or paramedic.

Before a suspect is asked to provide an intimate sample, they must be informed of the reason (including the nature of the suspected offence), that authorisation has been given and the provisions under which given, and that a sample taken at a police station may be subject of a speculative search. They must also be warned that, if they refuse without good cause, their refusal may harm their case if it comes to trial. If the suspect is in police detention and not legally represented, they must also be reminded of their entitlement to have free legal advice.

It should be noted that an intimate sample can only be taken with the written consent of the detainee and the authority of a senior police officer and, as such, blood and other intimate samples cannot be taken without consent nor can they be taken by force. I think it's also worth pointing out (particularly to those writers who may be looking to add some finer detail to their detention scenes) that, although semen is included in the list of intimate samples, this does not allow for the provision of semen samples by detainees!

Non-intimate sample
A non-intimate sample means:
(i)   a sample of hair, other than pubic hair, which includes hair plucked with the root;
(ii) a sample taken from a nail or from under a nail;
(iii) a swab taken from any part of a person's body other than a part from which a swab taken would be an intimate sample;
(iv) saliva;
(v)   a skin impression which means any record, other than a fingerprint, which is a record, in any form and produced by any method, of the skin pattern and other physical characteristics or features of the whole, or any part of, a person's foot or of any other part of their body.

Section 63 of the PACE Act provides that non-intimate samples may be taken from a person in police detention only with their written consent or without the appropriate consent in the following circumstances:

(a) under Section 63(2A) from a person who is in police detention as a consequence of being arrested for a recordable offence and who has not had a non-intimate sample of the same type and from the same part of the body taken in the course of the investigation of the offence by the police or they have had such a sample taken but it proved insufficient.

(b) Under Section 63(3) from a person who is being held in custody by the police on the authority of a court if an officer of at least the rank of Inspector authorises it to be taken.

An authorisation may be given:

(i) if the authorising officer has reasonable grounds for suspecting the person of involvement in a recordable offence and for believing that the sample will tend to confirm or disprove that involvement, and

(ii) in writing, or orally and confirmed in writing, as soon as practicable.

There are other sub-sections of Section 63 which relate to the taking of non-intimate samples when the person is not in police detention.

To summarise, an intimate sample can only be taken with the authority of an Inspector (or above) and the detainee's written consent. A non-intimate sample can be taken with the detainee's written consent or without their consent, providing it can be justified and is authorised by an Inspector (or above). Reasonable force may be used, if necessary, to take a non-intimate sample from a person without their consent.

Forensic sample examples

A man is arrested on suspicion of rape and detained at the police station. The investigating officer requires some samples in order to confirm or disprove the suspect's involvement in the offence. A sample of blood, pubic hair and penile swabs (intimate samples) are taken following the written consent of the detainee and the authority of the Duty Inspector. Swabs of the hands along with fingernail cuttings and scrapings (non-intimate samples) are taken following the written consent of the detainee. Without their consent it would still be possible to obtain the non-intimate samples (with the authority of an Inspector or above) but not the intimate samples.

Searches

If you have been arrested and are in police detention for an indictable offence (triable at Crown Court) the PACE Act (Section 18) provides the power to search premises which are occupied or controlled by the detained person. The written authority of an Inspector (or above) must be obtained and should only be given when the authorising officer is satisfied that the premises in question are actually occupied or controlled by the arrested person and that the necessary grounds exist. The authority and grounds will be recorded in the relevant custody record. The search is limited to evidence relating to the indictable offence for which the person has been arrested or another indictable offence which is similar or connected. The police will often simply refer to this type of search as a 'Section 18' and will usually carry out these searches at a person's home address. They can, however, also be carried out at a business premises or on a vehicle as long as these locations are controlled by the detainee and the appropriate authority is granted.

Section 18 search example
Bond is arrested for burglary and detained at the police station. There is property stolen from the burglary which has not been recovered and there is intelligence to suggest that Bond is responsible for other burglaries in the area. The investigating officer briefs the duty Inspector who authorises a Section 18 search of Bond's home address to search for the outstanding property stolen during the burglary and property which may have been stolen during other burglaries. During the search, a number of items are seized as they are believed to be stolen goods.

Interview
If you are in police detention for an offence which is being investigated, it's likely that you will be interviewed at some point. Prior to the introduction of the PACE Act in 1984 a police interview at the police station would probably have been contemporaneously recorded on paper. This process was time-consuming, open to abuse and often didn't result in an effective, free-flowing interview. PACE saw the introduction of the tape-recorded interview with the process being recorded onto two (sometimes three) audio cassette tapes. The sealed tapes would be taken into the interview room by the interviewing officer(s) and opened in the presence of the detained person (and their solicitor, if represented). Once the interview had concluded (or when the tape ran out if it was a lengthy interview) the tapes would be removed from the tape machine and placed back into their boxes. The interviewee would be asked to sign

an adhesive label which would be used to seal one of the tape boxes. This tape would be known as the 'master tape' and would only be opened if required at court or for some other exceptional reason. The remaining tape(s) would be referred to as the 'working tape' as, at some stage, the officer would probably have to listen to the interview and complete a written transcription of the relevant parts for a case file. The master tape would become a formal exhibit, referenced by the interviewing officer using their initials and a consecutive number. For example, if DC Stephen Morris had just interviewed a suspect on tape then the master tape would become exhibit SM/1. Sometimes an officer may also use their middle name initial as well (for example SJM/1), particularly during larger enquiries as there may be more than one person with the same two initials. If DC Morris had already referred to exhibits prior to the interview, the tape could become SM/3 or SM/4 etc, depending on the number of previous exhibits. During the last few years a lot of police forces have begun to use DVD's rather than cassette tapes and will also video record their interviews. The process is more or less the same with the sealing of discs as master copies unless the footage is recorded straight onto a hard drive or secure digital network.

Your interview may be conducted by a police officer or a member of police staff depending on the offence and the police force involved. At one time there would have been two interviewing officers but, unless the case is particularly serious, there is a possibility that there may now only be one interviewer. You will be given ample opportunity to consult privately with your solicitor (if represented) and will be provided with some information about the offence prior to the interview (known as pre-interview disclosure). Once the recording device is switched on and introductions have been completed, you will be cautioned before you are questioned. At any stage of the interview you can request a private consultation with your solicitor or a break. A lot of police interviews tend to be short but the more serious and complex cases can last for several hours and may be split into separate interviews.

Interviewing is a skill and a good interviewer is an asset to any criminal investigation. In murder investigations the interviewing pair will work as a team, not quite the 'good cop, bad cop' routine, but well-prepared and able to adapt if the interview doesn't go to plan. The interviewers will be Detective Constable's (DC) who are specially-trained for the role. An 'interview advisor' who will usually be a Detective Sergeant (DS) or possibly an experienced DC, will oversee the interview process remotely, briefing and de-briefing the interview team before and after each interview. If there are several suspects there may be a number of interview teams working simultaneously.

The vast majority of police interviews are carried out by DC's or sometimes DS's and, even though your TV dramas such as Midsomer Murders and Vera portray a different approach, the chances of a DI or DCI interviewing suspects at the police station are virtually nil. Having said that, I can perfectly understand why this happens as the episodes would be rather boring if the lead characters were stuck in the office or directing the investigation remotely which can often be the case in reality. Whilst I'm on the subject of police interviews portrayed on TV, I must mention the random uniformed officer who you'll always see standing in the corner or outside the interview room. Take a look and see if you can spot them next time you tune in. This is something which never happens in reality. There are alarm strips on the wall inside the interview room so that you can call for help should you need it and the only police officers present will be those conducting the interview.

Police interviews will start with a preamble from the interviewing officer before questions are put to the detainee.

Interview introduction example
"This interview is being audio (video) recorded and it may be given in evidence if your case is brought to trial. My name is DC Morris and I'm based at .... police station. I'm interviewing, can you state your full name for the purposes of the tape". (At this stage the detainee and others present will introduce themselves.) "The date is .... and the time by my watch is .... We're conducting this interview in Interview Room number ... at .... police station. At the end of the interview I'll explain how you can get a copy of the tapes". (If the detainee is not legally represented they should be reminded that they are entitled to free and independent legal advice and that the interview can be delayed so that they can obtain this advice.) "I must remind you that you are under caution and YOU DO NOT HAVE TO SAY ANYTHING BUT IT MAY HARM YOUR DEFENCE IF YOU DON'T MENTION WHEN QUESTIONED SOMETHING WHICH YOU LATER RELY ON IN COURT. ANYTHING YOU DO SAY MAY BE GIVEN IN EVIDENCE. Do you understand?"

If there is any doubt that the detainee may not understand the meaning of the caution, the interviewing officer should explain it in simplistic terms in their own words. Questioning will then begin. The questions should be put fairly and the behaviour of the interviewing officer(s) should be beyond reproach and not oppressive in any way.

CASE LAW (R v Miller 1992)

If police officers, when interviewing suspects, adopt hostile and intimidating techniques which render the interviews oppressive and confessions obtained unreliable, the court has no option but to exclude those confessions. A solicitor who is present during police interviews should responsibly and courageously discharge his function to intervene when improper questions are put. Police officers may be criticised for their interrogation techniques even if the solicitor has not intervened.

The appellants were convicted on 20th November 1990 of murdering a sex worker in Cardiff. Police interviews with Miller were central to the Crown's case against the appellants. Miller was interviewed on tape by the police over five days, for some thirteen hours. He denied both participation and presence at the murder scene well over 300 times during tapes 1–7 (of a total of 19). During tapes 8 and 9 he began to accept that he was present and eventually made three admissions that he had stabbed the victim. Miller appealed against conviction on the grounds that the interviews were oppressive and the whole course of questioning was such as to render his admissions unreliable and inadmissible under Section 76(2) of the Police and Criminal Evidence Act 1984.

During the appeal hearing the court had read the written transcripts of the case and heard a number of them played in open court. On hearing tape number 7 each member of the court was horrified as Miller was bullied and hectored. Short of physical violence, it was hard to conceive of a more hostile and intimidating approach by officers to a suspect. The solicitor present also appeared to have been at fault for sitting passively throughout the interview and not intervening.

Having considered the tenor and duration of the interviews taken as a whole, the court was of the opinion that they would have been oppressive and confessions obtained in consequence of them would have been unreliable. The interviews were central to the case against Miller and had been wrongly admitted in the original trial. The appeal was allowed and the verdicts delivered against the other two defendants (Paris and Abdullahi) were also regarded as unsafe.

In the circumstances of this case, the apparent failure of the provisions of the Police and Criminal Evidence Act 1984 to prevent evidence obtained by oppression and impropriety from being admitted did not indicate flaws in those provisions, more a combination of human errors.

The police officers adopted techniques of interrogation which were wholly contrary to the spirit and, in many instances, the letter of the codes laid down under the Act. If the interviewing officers took the view that unless and until the solicitor intervened they could not be criticised for going too far, they were wrong. Neither they nor the solicitor emerged from this case with any credit.

Conditions of detention

If you have been arrested and are detained in a police station for any length of time it's likely that you will be placed in a cell. These are very basic secure rooms with a toilet and a low bench which doubles as a bed. The cells are fitted with CCTV cameras which are monitored by the custody detention staff. The cell door will be heavy-duty and fitted with a hatch which can be pulled down to serve food/drink and to check on detainees. It will also probably be fitted with a spy-hole. During your detention you'll be provided with bedding and hot food and drink, served in plastic cartons and polystyrene cups. At least two light meals and one main meal should be offered in any 24-hour period. If your clothing has been taken from you, for the purposes of the investigation or for other good reason, you'll be supplied with replacement clothing which is normally a plain coloured tracksuit or similar. In any 24 hour period in custody you are entitled to eight hours rest free from interruption. Brief outdoor exercise should be offered daily if practicable. During your time in the cell you will be checked regularly by detention staff and, depending on your condition, you may be roused during these visits. It is rare for more than one person to be placed in the same cell but it does sometimes happen. A detailed risk assessment should be carried out before this decision is made and throughout the duration of the cell-share.

If you're writing a scene involving a character who is detained in a police cell or you just want to imagine what that might be like, I'll try to give you some idea. The cells are quite small and claustrophobic particularly once the door has been shut. The only natural light you may get will come from a series of small reinforced glass panes which you can't see clearly through as the glass is distorted. You will hear lots of noise, at all times of the day and night. It may be the rattling of keys and slamming of doors as cells are opened and closed, the squeaking of footwear as staff constantly walk around the cell corridors or the regular ringing of cell buzzers or alarms. More often than not, there will be someone detained who wants to shout at the top of their voice, try to talk to their 'mate' who's at the other end of the cell block or kick the inside of the cell door constantly. Peace and quiet is not something which the custody environment has the pleasure of experiencing very often. The smell of body odour, air freshener and the occasional waft of microwave 'all-day breakfast' or curry at meal times adds to the experience. The best way of describing it, particularly at peak times, is organised bedlam. The officers and staff who work in custody are in some of the most challenging roles in the police service.

Disposal

When your period of detention comes to an end, there are a number of different ways the police may dispose of you (figuratively rather than literally). This will depend on what, if any, evidence they have gathered and whether there are further enquiries required.

Charge

If there is sufficient evidence to provide a realistic prospect of a conviction then you may be charged with one or more offences. The charge(s) will probably be read out to you by the investigating officer at the custody desk and you will be cautioned. The caution upon charge is slightly different from the caution on arrest with the word 'now' replacing 'when questioned'. The caution upon charge is **'You do not have to say anything but it may harm your defence if you do not mention now something which you later rely on in court. Anything you do say may be given in evidence'**.

Once you have been charged you will either be remanded in custody or released on bail. The decision will be made by the custody Sergeant, taking into account a number of factors including the seriousness of the offence(s), your previous offending history and the likelihood of you interfering with witnesses, amongst others. If you are remanded into custody you will continue to be detained in a police cell until you are taken to the next available Magistrates court. If you are released on bail after charge you will be given a date, usually a few weeks later, when you must attend the Magistrates court for the case to be heard.

Crown Prosecution Service

At one time the police used to make their own decisions on charging but this role is now carried out by the Crown Prosecution Service (CPS). Each police force has its own local CPS branch and a working relationship with their case workers and lawyers. If a charging decision is required during office hours then the police will usually call their CPS branch and discuss the case with one of the lawyers. If a decision is required at night or at weekends then the police will contact CPS Direct, an out of hours service which provides charging decisions on priority cases. The officer will usually call a single national phone number to be connected to the next available Duty Prosecutor, one of a network of over 160 prosecutors based throughout England and Wales. After explaining the basic circumstances of the case, the officer will then send relevant case paperwork electronically to the CPS prosecutor who will review the case and provide a decision as to whether the detainee should be charged. CPS Direct only make the decision on whether to charge and, if so, the nature of the offence(s) and will probably have no further involvement in that case which will thereafter be handled by the local CPS branch. They provide a national 24 hour service for cases which require urgent advice.

Charging decision example

Baxter has been arrested for harassment and stalking his ex-partner. He has a previous conviction for a similar offence. He is arrested on Saturday afternoon and detained in custody whilst police investigate the circumstances. The investigating officer obtains a witness statement from the victim and one of the neighbours who saw and heard Baxter outside the victim's address. There is CCTV evidence which supports the case. Baxter makes 'no comment' to all questions put to him during police interviews. The following day, the police are in a position to seek charging advice from the CPS but, as it's a Sunday, their local branch is not available. The investigating officer contacts the out of hours service (CPS Direct) and provides the on-call lawyer with all relevant paperwork. A decision is made to charge Baxter with the offence of stalking and to refuse bail due to the circumstances. CPS Direct provide the investigating officer with an electronic copy of the charging decision which is included in the prosecution case file. Baxter is charged and remains in detention at the police station overnight until he is taken to the local Magistrates Court the following morning (Monday).

Release on police bail

For many years, if the police were not in a position to charge and needed to carry out further enquiries, await forensic results or prepare a file for CPS advice, they would release you on police bail, with or without conditions. In a number of cases, particularly child abuse and complex financial investigations, this could result in the suspected person being on bail for several months, perhaps even longer. The reasons for these delays were mainly due to limited specialist resources and the length of time it took to examine computers, other electronic devices and financial records. The lengthy periods on bail were often having an adverse effect on the mental health of those involved in cases which were not necessarily going to result in a charge.

The Policing and Crime Act 2017 has amended the bail provisions of the PACE Act to the effect that there is now a general presumption that if a person is released following their arrest it will be without bail. To release a person on bail the police must be satisfied that bail is necessary and proportionate in all the circumstances. Any release on bail should, in most cases, be for no longer than 28 days and must be authorised by an officer of at least Inspector rank. In a Serious Fraud Office (SFO) case this period could be up to three months rather than 28 days. In all other cases the period of bail can be extended from 28 days to three months if certain conditions are met and only when authorised by a senior police officer (of Superintendent rank or above).

Pre-charge bail may be extended to a point 6 months after arrest if a case has been designated as 'exceptionally complex' by a senior prosecutor and only when authorised by a police officer of at least the rank of Assistant Chief Constable (Commander in the Metropolitan or City of London forces). Although these exceptions are in place, the majority of cases won't be subject to pre-charge bail but if they are, it is likely to be for no more than 28 days.

Release under investigation (RUI)

This is a relatively recent category of disposal which was designed to address the situation of lengthy periods on police bail. If you are now 'released under investigation' then you will not be given a date to return to the police station and you will not be bound by the terms and conditions of police bail. Once all enquiries have been completed and a decision has been made you will be notified by the police. You may have to attend the police station to be interviewed and you may be re-arrested if new evidence comes to light. On the other hand, you may be informed that no further action is being taken.

Although this approach was introduced to prevent lengthy delays on bail it has been subject to criticism from some legal firms who are of the view that removing investigatory deadlines has resulted in police officers being less expeditious during their investigations.

CASE STUDY – RELEASED UNDER INVESTIGATION
Figures released in early 2020 show that nationally 80% of suspects arrested are released under investigation. The average amount of time spent whilst RUI before a decision was made was 139 days (the average length on police bail prior to the reforms was 90 days). Some cases take far longer. The London Criminal Courts Solicitors' Association recently reported that, in a sample of RUI cases, more than 69 had been ongoing for between 18 months and two years.

One such example arose in early 2020 at Sheffield Crown Court during the sentencing of a man convicted of supplying Class A drugs. The Judge's remarks were widely published and critical of the police and CPS for a period of almost two years between the arrest of the suspect and eventual charge. An aggravating factor was the apparent strength of the evidence which made the lengthy delay even more puzzling. The Judge observed that "the police did nothing, they did absolutely nothing for 11 months" resulting in a delay which left the defendant "hanging" for almost two years to learn his fate. The issues with RUI have been acknowledged by the Government which announced in November 2019 that a review would take place. In 2017–18 there were more than 193,000 people RUI as the number of people bailed fell considerably. There is merit in such an approach but the use of RUI must be closely monitored and not allowed to fall into disrepute.

Release without charge (RWOC)

If it is clear that there is no evidence to support a charge and that further enquiries would be unlikely to identify such evidence than you may be released without charge. This means that no further action will be taken against you and there is no need for you to return to the police station at a future date. If however, new evidence comes to light in relation to the same matter then it's possible that you could be arrested again and detained for the purposes of the investigation. Examples of when a person may be RWOC could involve a case of mistaken identity or where enquiries reveal that the person hasn't actually committed the offence they were suspected of, or any other criminal offence.

Custody detention example

Wilson is arrested on suspicion of attempted murder after he was named as being responsible for stabbing another man several times earlier that day. Part of the incident was captured on CCTV. He arrives at the police station at 5.15pm (the 'relevant time') and is taken to the custody reception area. Fortunately, there is no queue and the arresting officer is able to take him straight to the desk. The officer provides the grounds and reason for arrest to the custody Sergeant who authorises detention at 5.25pm to secure and preserve evidence and to obtain evidence by questioning. His personal details are taken and a computerised custody record is created. As part of this process a risk assessment is carried out, with Wilson being asked a series of questions about his health and welfare. It is established that he does not present a risk at that time to himself or others. He is over 18 and does not require an appropriate adult. He is searched and a number of items are seized for evidence and safekeeping. He is informed of his rights, choosing not to have anyone informed of his arrest but requesting the duty solicitor.

Wilson is then taken to a private side room where his outer clothing and footwear are seized as evidence. He is given police-issue clothing and footwear. His fingerprints are digitally scanned, his photograph is taken and a sample of his DNA is obtained by way of a buccal mouth-swab. Due to the circumstances of the incident, the investigating officer requests some intimate and non-intimate samples from Wilson in the form of blood samples (for drugs/alcohol content and DNA) and swabs from his hands. Wilson agrees to provide these samples and confirms his consent in writing on the custody record. The request to obtain intimate samples of blood is authorised by the Duty Inspector. A doctor attends the police station to take the samples.

The weapon which is believed to have been used by Wilson to inflict the injuries hasn't been recovered and the police would like to search his home address to see if it is there and to see if there is any other evidence connected to the offence. Authority is granted under Section 18 PACE Act by the Duty Inspector and noted on the custody record. During the search, a total of three knives are found and brought back to the police station for potential forensic examination. No other items of interest are found during the search.

When the duty solicitor arrives at the police station he is allowed to examine Wilson's custody record then has a private consultation with his client in an interview room. The investigating officer provides the solicitor with written pre-interview disclosure and, following a further private consultation, Wilson is interviewed by police. His solicitor reads out a pre-prepared written statement from Wilson claiming that he acted in self-defence. Wilson makes 'no comment' to all further questions.

At 11.25pm (six hours after his detention was first authorised) the first review of detention is carried out by the night duty Inspector. After the review, Wilson is returned to his cell where he is placed into an eight hour rest period free from interruption.

The following morning, Wilson has breakfast and at 8.25am (nine hours after the first review) a second review of his detention is carried out by the Duty Inspector. Police enquiries continue throughout the day and it becomes clear that the investigating officer is going to need to apply to keep Wilson in detention without charge for more than 24 hours. The officer discusses the investigation with the local Superintendent, explaining outstanding enquiries and outlining the reasons why the extension is necessary. The investigating officer requests an additional 12 hour extension, beyond 24 hours. The Superintendent hears representations from Wilson's solicitor and, satisfied that the investigation is being conducted diligently and expeditiously, authorises an additional 8 hour extension beyond 24 hours. She informs Wilson and his solicitor then updates the custody record accordingly.

At 5.25pm a third review of detention is carried out by the Duty Inspector as Wilson has now been in custody for 24 hours. At this point the extension of detention authorised by the local Superintendent begins.

During the course of the day the police have gathered additional evidence from witnesses, CCTV and mobile phone data. This evidence is put to Wilson in further interviews. He maintains 'no comment' and declines to add to the prepared statement claiming self-defence.

The police believe that they now have sufficient evidence to charge Wilson and, due to the serious nature of the offence, think that a remand in custody would be appropriate. Due to the time of day, the local CPS branch is no longer available, so the investigating officer contacts the out of hours service (CPS Direct) to request a charging decision. After reviewing the relevant documentation, the on-call lawyer advises charges of unlawful wounding with intent and possession of a knife in a public place. Wilson is subsequently charged with the two offences and remanded in police detention by the custody Sergeant due to the serious nature of the charges and his previous offending history.

Wilson remains in detention at the police station after charge until he is taken to the local Magistrates court the following morning. Post-charge reviews of his detention are carried out by the custody Sergeant in accordance with PACE.

The Authors' Reflections on the Topic

Stuart Gibbon

Once again, as with the subject of arrest, the introduction of the Police and Criminal Evidence Act 1984 provided a legislative framework and a detailed Codes of Practice for police officers in relation to the detention, treatment and questioning of suspects.

Prior to this, the practice of police officers, often detectives, interviewing suspects at length without proper representation, using oppressive tactics during lengthy interviews or leaving them in a cell for unreasonable amounts of time was not uncommon. Attempts to investigate police corruption were often thwarted by intervention or obstruction from within. Although PACE wasn't fully enacted until 1986, its introduction certainly helped address a lot of the malpractice identified in previous decades. Tape-recorded interviews rather than handwritten contemporaneous notes, specific rights for detainees and strict timescales in relation to detention were a step in the right direction. Further legislation and police training, particularly in relation to interviewing techniques, has also transformed the way that police detention is managed. I can say, with a degree of confidence, that the well-documented miscarriages of justice related to the detention and treatment of people in police custody would not happen today, nor during recent years.

During my police career, I was lucky enough to have the opportunity to carry out many different roles including uniformed response, public protection and murder investigation. All were challenging and carried a degree of risk which you expect as a police officer. My time spent as a custody Sergeant is right up there and will always be a role I have the utmost respect for. It tends to be a position which some colleagues may take for granted but is, without doubt, one of the most important roles in any force. It's also probably one of the most stressful, as you constantly try to manage the demands of a busy custody suite whilst keeping everyone safe. Without custody sergeants and their detention staff, the police service would simply grind to a halt so I'd like to pay tribute to the invaluable work they all do.

Stephen Wade

The world's great writers have made much of illegal detention; without the concept, literature would be the poorer. R L Stevenson, in his novel, *Catriona*, made this abuse a pivotal feature of the thriller strand in his story. The clearest instance of exactly what the issues are is perhaps in chapter XIV when Black Andie, jailer to the hero, listens to the truth of what he is doing:

> *To be apprehended by some ragged John-Hielandmen on August 30th, carried to a rickle* of old stones that is now neither fort nor gaol... but just the gamekeeper's lodge of the Bass Rock, and set free again, September 23rd, as secretly as I was first arrested – does that sound like law to you? or does it sound like justice? *A pile or heap*

From my viewpoint as a historian primarily concerned with the years *c*.1700–1920, the subject of arrest and detention has changed from areas of criminal law related to crime as it integrates into society and social dilemmas, through to international complexities about territory, displacement and a dynamic fusion of law and morality in borderlands across the world.

Law and morality have always been partners, locked together like twins, and in any given society, their interplay in a criminal prosecution will become enlightening for readers and researchers. On our television screens every day we see images of people on the run across borders, fleeing from war and persecution. This has always happened, right through history, but never so transparently. In 1900, British travellers were revolted by the sight, in China, of prisoners caged like poultry in a market-place. Never had they seen such a form of detention before. It was even more abhorrent than the medieval 'oubliette' in which the poor victim was thrown into a tiny dungeon, with no rights expressed.

The other main conclusion I have to reflect on is the sheer length of time, in Britain's criminal history, that a prisoner had to wait before trial in the assize system. Because the travelling justices arrived in town twice a year, the jails were packed with the accused awaiting trial. The justices' duty was *'oyez and terminez'* – to clear the prisons and pass sentences. But the county prisons back in Georgian times were so riddled with disease that many people, awaiting trial and therefore un-convicted, died (often of typhus) in their cells.

Bibliography

Works Cited

Bagley, J.J., *Historical Interpretation Volume 1 Sources of English Medieval History 1066–1540* (Penguin, 1971)

Connor, Paul, *et alia Blackstone's Police Manuals 2020* (OUP, 2020)

Costin, W.C., and Watson, J. Steven, *The Law and Working of the Constitution: Documents 1660–1914* (Adam and Charles Black, 1952)

Gatrell, Vic, *City of Laughter: sex and satire in eighteenth century London* (Atlantic Books, 2006)

Gilbert, Michael, (Editor) *The Oxford Book of Legal Anecdotes* (OUP, 1986)

Halliday, Paul D., *Habeas Corpus* (Belknap Press, 2010)

Saunders, John B., *Mozley and Whiteley's Law Dictionary* (Butterworths, 1977)

Scotland, Lt.Col. A.P., *The London Cage* (Evans Brothers, 1957)

Steedman, Carolyn, *The Radical Soldier's Tale: John Pearman, 1819–1908* (Routledge, 1988)

Stevenson, Robert Louis, *Catriona* (OUP 1986)

Thomas, Donald, *State Trials Vol. 2 The Public Conscience* (Routledge, 1972)

Reference Works

Baker, J. H., *An Introduction to English Legal History* (Butterworths, 2002)

Cowie, L.W., *The Wordsworth Dictionary of British Social History* (Wordsworth, 1973)

Morris, Norval, and Rothman, David J., *The Oxford History of the Prison* (OUP, 1998)

Essays and Articles

Harvey, Katherine, 'The Unfamiliar King' *Time Literary Supplement* July 3 2020 p. 7

Law Report February 18 2020 'Wrongful Imposition of a Curfew Amounts to False Imprisonment' *The Times* p. 55

Melechi, Anthony, 'The Sound of Blood Rushing' in *Time Literary Supplement* July 3 2020 p. 14

Internet Sources

CCRC Criminal Cases Review Commission

Discovery.nationalarchives.gov.uk

Chancery Files, Tower Series

Go.gale.com>i.do

Heinonline.org – 'Habeas Corpus Cum Causa – The Emergence of the Modern Writ.'

www.amnesty.org.uk – Human Rights Law

www.libertyhumanrights.org.uk – Human Rights Act – Liberty

GUIDE TO FURTHER READING

The literature of detention and imprisonment is immense. Not only is this body of work infused with unspeakable and inhuman instances of abuse in terms of the exercise of power, but also, in the area of torture, which is often linked to detention as a major issue. I am writing this in the summer of 2020 and I am still reflecting on a visit I made to York in March. Walking in the tourist attraction of The Shambles, I passed the shrine dedicated to Saint Margaret Clitherow. Back in 1586, being prosecuted for offences linked to her faith, because she would not plead, she was sentenced to be 'pressed' until dead. That terrible fate awaited her, and to make the whole situation worse, she was detained in a tiny stone block on one of the bridges over the Ouse. Such, at certain times, can be the brutality of the law.

Our introduction has of course been a minimal treatment of the topics; that is the intention of the series. But we have given the salient points of two very complex concepts in law. Had we gone into a wider enquiry, the ground covered would have included international law, and a great deal of material on law and morality. After all, a state's legal structures reflect not only an ideology but a vision of the world and its power structures at one end of the spectrum, and then the regulation and control of personal behaviour and alignment with the social contract on the other.

With this in mind, we have restricted the topics and our treatment of them to the more familiar context which will be encountered by readers of British true crime and crime history. But a consideration of further reading opens up some of these grander, more comprehensive areas of enquiry, particularly in international law, which is beyond the scope of the present volume.

The twenty-first century has seen unprecedented challenges to former concepts of detention, as global crime, population movements and mass communications have all had their impact of why and how detention should take place. Of course, many of the modern instances in this regard are not criminal detention, and so the waters become muddied.

For the historical contexts regarding detention, there is an abundance of riches available. Academia is taking more and more interest in the history of crime, as the social science of criminology becomes increasingly attractive to undergraduates, and to postgraduates who select a specific area of law or forensics to examine. J H Baker's history (see above in the bibliography) is the place to start. The following is therefore a short, selected listing.

General
Denning, Lord, *Landmarks in the Law* (Butterworths, 1984)
De Than, Claire, *Law Express: Human Rights* (Pearson, 2018)
Gibson, B., *Human Rights and the Courts* (Waterside Press, 200)
Rivlin, Geoffrey, *Understanding the Law* Fifth edition (OUP, 2009)
Tomlins, T.E., & Brown, Josiah, *Reports of cases upon appeals and writs or error determined in the High Court of Parliament* (A. Strahan, 1803)
Human Rights and Detention: Hill-Cawthorne, Lawrence, *Detention in Non-International Armed Conflict* (OUP, 2020)
Weisburd, A.Mark, *Comparative Human Rights Law: Detention, Prosecution, Capital Punishment* (Carolina Academic Press, 2008)

Police Work:

Donoghue, John, Police: *Arrests and Suspects: the true story of a front-line officer* (Matador, 2015)

Smart, Huw, *Blackstone's Custody Officers' Manual* (OUP, 2019)

Preventive Detention:

Frankowski, Stanislav, *Preventive Detention: A comparative and international law perspective* (Springer, 1992)

Webber, Diane, *Preventive Detention of Terror Suspects* (Routledge, 2018)

Historical

Anon. *Reports from the Commissioner, Inspectors and Others Vol. XXXIX* (HMSO 1896)

Cumming, Sir John, *Bibliography Dealing with Crime and Cognate Subjects (*Receiver for the Metropolitan Police District, 1935)

Lawson, John D., (Ed) *American State Trials* (Thomas Law Book Co., 1914)

Mandler, Peter, (Ed) *Liberty and Authority in Victorian England* (OUP., 2006)

Ross, John M., *Trials in Collections: an index to famous trials throughout the world* (Scarecrow Press, 1983)

Scott, Sir Harold, *The Concise Encyclopaedia of Crime and Criminals* (Andre Deutsch, 1961)

Stammers, Neil, *Civil Liberties in Britain During the Second World War* (Croom Helm, 1983)

Zedner, Lucia, *Women, Crime and Custody in Victorian England* (OUP, 1994)

INDEX

Reviews for Previous Books by
Stephen Wade and Stuart Gibbon

THE CRIME WRITER'S CASEBOOK

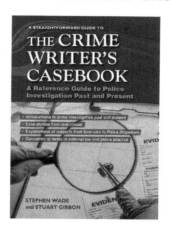

A fantastic addition to any crime writer's bookshelf!

Caroline Mitchell – Bestselling author

What a massive compilation of facts this book is – a must for anyone writing crime. Everything that you need to know, expertly indexed for ease of reference.

Pam Fish – National Association of Writer's Groups (NAWG)

This is a comprehensive and well-written guide for anyone wanting to write a realistic crime novel or a non-fiction work involving police operations.

Police History Society Magazine June 2018

If you're thinking of writing crime or crime thriller and wondering where to start, then 'The Crime Writer's Casebook' is an absolute must-have reference book. With case studies from real crimes, explanations of forensics and police procedure from leading experts in their fields and an understandable A-Z index of legal terms, it's every bit the straightforward guide it claims to be. Pick a subject you need information on, flick to the index, and you will find it. It's all there. Anything you need, you have it at your fingertips. Browsing the index itself got my writing juices flowing. I'm actually not sure how I managed without it. I honestly cannot recommend this gem of a reference book enough.

Sheryl Browne – Bestselling author

This book was recommended by author CL Taylor. One of the authors, Stuart Gibbon – a former DCI, has consulted on her best-selling crime novels for many years. This book is everything I expected and far more. Gibbon's in-depth knowledge and experience of policing alongside Wade's well researched and detailed references to historical crimes make this a must-read, whether you are a reader or writer of true crime or crime fiction. I am currently using this guide to help with the research for my debut novel. The information on forensics and police procedure, alongside case studies and facts about the law, is invaluable. Gibbon and Wade have packed an enormous amount of information into this guide, which is not only fascinating and insightful, but also incredibly practical and easy to use. I look forward to reading book two, 'Being a Detective'.

Samantha – UK Crime Book Club

BEING A DETECTIVE

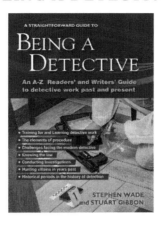

A fascinating insight into detective work, both in the past and right now. So useful for crime writers but also really interesting for anyone interested in police work generally. Simple clear language and great use of real life case studies to illustrate various points. A great companion to the authors' previous work, 'The Crime Writers' Casebook'.

Jackie Kabler – TV presenter and crime writer

After devouring 'The Crime Writer's Casebook', the first book by ex-Metropolitan Police Detective Stuart Gibbon and crime historian Stephen Wade, I was extremely excited to read 'Being a Detective'. And it didn't disappoint one iota. If you're like me, a crime addict, whether that be for crime fiction novels or those addictive true crime documentaries on Netflix, this is the perfect book to have on your shelf. It's bursting with information, everything you could possibly want to know is in these books.

Ronnie Turner – Author and Book Blogger

There are no words to describe the marvellousness of this book. It's a must asset for the crime writer. It gives a wonderful insight into the world of detectives and the difficult job they do. I felt having both authors in my living room as if they were present narrating me their special skills. A wonderful work full of technicalities which are a must-know for the writer who wishes to give a plausible brushing on his work. It's the second co-operation between the authors, after their book "The Crime Writer's Casebook" and I was amazed by the different perspectives and new information I got. I highly recommend it.

FloBell (reviewed in Germany)

I cannot stress how useful and informative this book is! As a crime writer, I keep it close at hand and use it often. I would definitely recommend it to anyone interested in the way police operate, writers of crime or aspiring crime writers. I love this book and it's a good way of ensuring that your work has an authentic air about it.

Griffy

A brilliant follow up book with even more amazing inside detail on being a detective. An essential part of any crime or thriller writer's library.

MR